Answering the Call

Answering the Call

*How God Transformed the Lives
of Nineteen Catholic Deacons*

MICHAEL J. MCGRATH
EDITOR

RESOURCE *Publications* · Eugene, Oregon

ANSWERING THE CALL
How God Transformed the Lives of Nineteen Catholic Deacons

Copyright © 2010 Michael J. McGrath. All rights reserved. Except for brief quotations in critical publications or reviews, no part of this book may be reproduced in any manner without prior written permission from the publisher. Write: Permissions, Wipf and Stock Publishers, 199 W. 8th Ave., Suite 3, Eugene, OR 97401.

Resource Publications
An Imprint of Wipf and Stock Publishers
199 W. 8th Ave., Suite 3
Eugene, OR 97401
www.wipfandstock.com

ISBN 13: 978-1-60608-948-4

Manufactured in the U.S.A.

All scripture quotations, unless otherwise indicated, are taken from the Holy Bible, New International Version®, NIV®. Copyright ©1973, 1978, 1984 by Biblica, Inc.™ Used by permission of Zondervan. All rights reserved worldwide.

Contents

Preface vii
List of Abbreviations xiii
Contributors xv
Introduction xix

Deacon J. Brian Bergeron 1

Deacon John Blaha 5

Deacon Tirso A. Castillo 12

Deacon Jerry Clark 26

Deacon Don Coates 38

Deacon Kerry Diver 45

Deacon Tom Eden 61

Deacon Peter Falkenhausen 71

Deacon Richard Halbur 79

Deacon Dave Hayden 83

Deacon Bob Kepshire 88

Deacon Ken Maleck 101

Deacon Michael J. McGrath 107

Deacon Patrick Mongan 114

Deacon Reinaldo Morales 123

Deacon Bienvenido Perez, Jr. 131

Deacon James Roberge 142

Deacon Joseph S. Soparas 151

Deacon Albert Sullivan 158

Epilogue 163

Reverend Michael W. Cooper, S.J., S.T.D.
St. Leo University (Florida)

Preface

ON THE WALL IN my office at Saint Leo University hangs a Testimonial Plaque from the Savannah Diaconate Class of 2008. You will soon have the joy of reading the essays on ministry of nineteen of them. This testimonial reminds me of the great joy and satisfaction I experienced as I watched them grow together as brothers, as well as very competent ministers of the Gospel, through our spiritual and academic journey over six years. At the heart of this journey lies the deep friendships and close bond we have for each other, whether we see each other physically or not.

I often share my belief and trust in my brothers by saying I know any of them would stand up with me and for me, and I would do the same for any of them. The bonds of friendship we share with each other and "in the Lord Jesus" remain truly "the great gift beyond price."

I remember our first class on a Friday evening in the parish hall of Immaculate Conception Catholic Church in Dublin, Georgia to begin the Aspirancy Year of spiritual formation. Few of the then twenty-nine men and their wives knew each other. As couples sat silently at the round tables waiting for things to start, a lot of questions were running around in peoples' minds. Who are these other men? What are they like and will we get along? Am I smart enough? Am I worthy? Sitting in the back of the room was "a Deacon's Deacon," George Foster, and his very loving wife, Georgia. Perhaps the one thing many of the men had in common that evening was a friendship and admiration of George. He was the reason many of them were there. Through our journey over six years, we all realized more and more that George is "a Deacon's Deacon," and together, George and Georgia epitomize what it means to be "a deacon couple," sharing love, faith, and ministry together—for us.

With my high-energy, extroverted teaching style laced with a good bit of humor, we began. I explained the importance of this Aspirancy Year dedicated to spiritual development before beginning the academic rigors of the Master of Arts in Pastoral Studies (MAPS) through Saint Leo University. As I reflect, I can say without hesitancy that, "We did it right!" I have absolute trust in the pastoral, theological, and spiritual ministries of these men, who are often joined by their wives in ministry. As you read their essays, you will see for yourself what gifted ministers they are. The success of the Master of Arts in Pastoral Studies Program for these deacons comes from the excellent Saint Leo professors and from the solid spiritual formation they began during the Aspirancy Year. Several of the essays state that very explicitly. The Lord was very powerful, walking with each of these men and helping them face and overcome fears and hurts to discover that they are each loved by God as they are. Moreover, they are gifted and able to find God in all things, because they know firsthand that God goes looking for and finds them in any and every situation. Many discovered not only a personal friendship with the Lord but also an apostolic, world-embracing spirituality for their life and ministry in the Church and in the world. Ultimately, the success of this program lies in the wisdom and leadership of Deacon George Foster, who supported and fought for a full year of spiritual formation, which resulted in these men being well grounded in themselves, in one another, and in the Lord. From this spiritual base came a living synthesis of theology, spirituality, and ministry. Yes, we did it right!

For the sake of posterity and to offer other formation programs the wisdom of our efforts, I would like to take the second half of this Preface to describe the elements of the Aspirancy Year in detail. As a Jesuit involved both in the ministries of university teaching spiritual direction and from my personal experience, I knew that the "Retreat in Everyday Life," the Spiritual Exercises of Ignatius Loyola done over the course of six-eight months, offered the best structure on which to build this Aspirancy Year. We chose: *Moment by Moment: A Retreat in Everyday Life* (Notre Dame; Ave Maria Press, 2000), developed at Marquette University by Father Gene F. Merz, S. J. and Carol Ann Smith, SHCJ. This adapted journey through the Spiritual Exercises contains relevant texts from the Exercises, biblical suggestions for prayer, and suggestive reflection questions to help stay with the unfolding process. Each aspirant and spouse were asked to pray more or less an hour a day and spend another half-hour or so on the reflection questions and journaling. As with many of the "requirements," there was initially some resistance and occasional confusion about what was being asked. The almost immediate power and fruitfulness of these spiritual exercises calmed the fears and anxieties, and encouraged people to stay with the process.

Each retreatant was gradually introduced to the "Examen of Consciousness," reinterpreted by George Aschenbrenner, S.J., as an exercise in daily discernment of where is the Lord in my life and how have I responded. Each aspirant was also asked to get a spiritual director and meet with that person every two weeks. Most had no idea what spiritual direction was or how to find a spiritual director. I explained that the director was not to tell someone what to do, but rather to listen and to help the retreatant to process and deepen the prayer and reflection during the retreat. The spiritual director was not the same as a confessor nor should it be one's best friend or prayer partner. This wisdom figure needs to have some distance and objectivity in order to accompany the retreatant. The director could be a priest, deacon, or a lay person—male or female, but someone who could listen well and not interfere by trying to direct or control the process. I daresay that once the process got going, many retreatants wondered how they had gotten by before without a spiritual director. Again, the fruitfulness and wisdom of these sessions and the chance to process issues and questions that came up in life or in prayer became the gift of great price. I presume today that most of the class continues to see their spiritual director on a regular basis.

Each aspirant and their spouse were also asked to join with 3-4 other couples every two weeks for "faith sharing." Through their sharing what God was saying and doing during their retreat and in their everyday lives, these small groups served as a way to experience how God deals differently with each person and to support one another on the journey. These "small community" experiences in faith-sharing proved to be great builders of trust and ongoing friendship among the whole group, as well as for the particular small group. The mini-gatherings also allowed those who were not as comfortable sharing in the larger group during the weekends to voice their experience of the Lord comfortably. Thus, on alternate weeks, the aspirants were either seeing their spiritual director or meeting with their small faith-sharing group—a fairly intense schedule which proved invaluable for all the blessings and community belonging it fostered.

Each aspirant received three hours of graduate or undergraduate credit for REL 582: Finding God in All Things: The Apostolic and World-Embracing Spirituality of Ignatius Loyola. Once a month, we met on Friday evenings and all day Saturday, ending with Eucharist together at 3 p.m. During the weekends, we would process theologically, spiritually, and ministerially the four "Moments" we had been working on during the month. In addition, we had lectures and discussions on the handouts, articles, and two books we used on spiritual growth and development from an Ignatian and Vatican II perspective. William Creed, S.J.,'s (available online from the author) offers an excellent understanding of the Exercises—especially his chapters on discernment of spirits. Gerald R. Grosh, S.J.,'s (out of print but available from Fr. Cooper) presents excellent case studies of developmental stages of psychological and spiritual growth.

As part of the academic requirements, we used WebCT, a learning management system for ongoing discussion during the weeks when we were not physically present in Dublin. Dr. Caroline Cerveny, S.S.J., D. Min, who helped design the MAPS program, brought her expertise in educational technology for ministry to setting up and helping all of us use WebCT. We divided the students into three separate discussion groups and every week had an opening reflection question related to the Moment for that week. The participants were expected to post 3-5 times per week and interact with the others in their group. Initially, a number of the students were not that comfortable with computers and technology. Some even fought it. Several, however, were very competent and helped the others get on board—another experience of brotherhood and of empowering each other.

Sister Caroline offered the next course in our sequence, REL 560: CyberCulture: New Challenges for Pastoral Ministry, where everyone had to get a laptop to take advantage of the wireless capabilities of the parish hall in Dublin. Despite some expected and unexpected glitches, Sister Caroline exercised her masterful teaching skills and her command of technology's applications for ministry to advance our aspirants' familiarity and comfort with the Internet for diaconal service. Again, some who fought the hardest became the greatest disciples. I personally witnessed their final projects—websites for their parishes, a Power Point presentation for a Spanish RCIA program, a training program for altar servers, the history of a parish, and many more which you will hear about in some of the essays. Again, thanks to the support of Deacon Foster and Dr. Douglas Astolfi, then Vice-President of Academic Affairs at Saint Leo, who believed in the role of technology in ministry for the twenty-first century, "we did it right." This diaconate class remains the most comfortable and astute in the applications of the Internet and the use of technology in ministry.

The aspirants posted their comments and interacted with each other. As the professor of record, I had access to the conversation of each of the three groups and basically responded to every posting. The postings documented, if you will, personal applications of the Spiritual Exercises and the spiritual development material. On many occasions, we were all surprised and moved by the wisdom and profound insights shared by the participants. Again, "we did it right!" WebCT remained a powerful learning tool as well as a community builder in the weeks when we were not meeting.

Finally, each student had to do three five-page, single-spaced reflection papers to name and integrate more deeply what they were learning spiritually, theologically, and pastorally. I made extensive comments on their papers and returned them. Because I live in the Tampa Bay area, I followed up with a face-to-face conversation on the weekend or by a phone call. Obviously, these efforts were very labor-intensive but made for an excellent learning experience as well as real bonding between us.

The Aspirancy Year of spiritual formation brought a multitude of gifts and offered a faith-filled foundation in the Lord that integrated the courses that followed. Through "the Retreat in Everyday Life" and the material on spiritual growth and development through an Ignatian and Vatican II perspective, the aspirants faced some of their fears and wounds, and even sin, and came to know deep down that they are loved by God as they are. They also discovered the spirituality of weakness through Michael Buckley, S.J.,'s masterpiece of the spiritual life, "Because Beset By Weakness." They prayed and shared on their individual and particular gifts and heard Christ call them personally and by name to share his Mission today. Their personal friendship with Jesus allowed them to face "death and dying in everyday life." Knowing intimately through the Paschal Mystery of the Death and Resurrection of Jesus, they can wait and minister in hope and trust that "out of these daily deaths, God does open up new life, new hope, new possibilities in amazing and unexpected ways." Sorrow, hurts, wounds, evil, and even sin are never the last Word but always New Life, Resurrection in the Risen Lord. They have learned to follow the lead of the Spirit in their life and ministry through daily discernment of spirits using the Examen of Consciousness and applying the experiential rules or guidelines for "Discernment of Spirits" from Ignatius of Loyola. The result of this year of spiritual formation is an apostolic, world-embracing spirituality of "finding God in all things" or, in the words of Karl Rahner, S.J., "the mysticism of everyday life."

As I do an "Ignatian repetition" of the gifts and graces of this Aspirancy Year and of the years and courses that followed, I am incredibly moved by how these men have affected me and how our shared friendship and faith in the Lord remain such a powerful bulwark in my own life and ministry. I am also most appreciative of my deep friendship with Deacon George and Georgia Foster—a great gift in all ways. In both the Aspirancy Year and in the final course on "The Theology and Spirituality of Ministry," I regularly called upon George in class for support and wisdom in some of the difficult and challenging issues that came up. I hope my reflections here help you to enter more deeply into the wisdom and spirituality for ministry of these Savannah deacons, my band of brothers.

Michael W. Cooper, S.J., S.T.D.
September 9, 2009

Abbreviations of Books of the Bible

Gen	Genesis
Exod	Exodus
Lev	Leviticus
Deut	Deuteronomy
Josh	Joshua
Kgs	Kings
Ps	Psalm
Isa	Isaiah
Jer	Jeremiah
Ezek	Ezekiel
Mic	Micah
Matt	Matthew
Rom	Romans
Cor	Corinthians
Gal	Galatians
Eph	Ephesians
Col	Colossians
Tim	Timothy
Jas	James
Pet	Peter
Sir	Sirach

Contributors

Deacon J. Brian Bergeron and Jill, his wife of twenty-one years, have two daughters, Alexa and Abby. Deacon J. Brian has an extremely active ministry at Our Divine Saviour Catholic Church (Tifton, GA) and its mission church, St. Ann's (Alapaha, GA). Deacon J. Brian also travels with his enthusiastic ministry, Jesus Rocks (www.jesusrocksministry.com). He is a professional salesman and entrepreneur.

Deacon John D. Blaha and his wife Trish are the parents of a combined family of five children. Deacon John is assigned to St. Augustine Catholic Church in Thomasville, GA. He is semi-retired.

Deacon Tirso Castillo and his wife Annette live in Dublin, Georgia. They are the parents of three children. Deacon Tirso is a full-time gastroenterologist and serves Immaculate Conception Church in Dublin. In addition to balancing the demands of being a dad, a doctor, and a deacon, Deacon Tirso also manages a forty-acre hay field.

Deacon Jerry Clark and his wife Judy are members of Saint Frances Cabini in Savannah, GA. They have two children and seven grandchildren. Deacon Jerry's ministries outside the Parish include prison, hospital, and visiting the sick and shut-ins. In the private sector, he is Director of IT for a paper manufacturer.

Deacon Don Coates and his wife Karen are Catholic school educators and the parents of three children: Reeves, Brooks, and Katie (Bert). Karen teaches fourth grade (Saint Joseph; Macon, GA), and Don is the Campus Minister for Mount de Sales Academy, where he plans Masses and all liturgical services. In his parish, Don also serves as the Deacon for Latin Masses.

Father Michael Cooper, S.J. is a Jesuit priest with a doctorate in theology from the Institut Catholique in Paris. For nearly forty years he has combined university teaching in the areas of spirituality, pastoral studies, and systematic theology with pastoral ministry. His pastoral work includes spiritual direction, personally-directed and preached retreats, and workshops. He is presently a professor at Saint Leo University.

Deacon Kerry Diver and his wife Verna serve the parish of St. Teresa of Avila in Grovetown, GA. They have one son, Steven, who is a college student. The deacon couple direct RCIA and are involved in adult education. Deacon Kerry is a physician and Verna, a former dentist, teaches Anatomy and Physiology at Augusta State University.

Deacon Tom Eden and his wife Thalia, a school counselor, have three grown sons. After a sales and general management business career in the Northeast, Central and West Coast, they now reside in Macon, GA. Tom is a ministry business manager, university business teacher and deacon serving low-income families and people with addictions.

Deacon Pete Falkenhausen and his wife Cathy are parents of four children: Brittany, Katie, Peter, and Thomas. Deacon Pete and Cathy serve the parish of St. John the Evangelist Catholic Church (Valdosta, GA). He is the Chief of Weapons Safety at Moody AFB, GA and a retired USAF Master Sergeant.

Deacon George H. Foster and his wife Georgia have been married for fifty-seven years. They have six children, thirteen grandchildren and two great-grandchildren. Deacon George is the Director of the Permanent Diaconate Program for the Diocese of Savannah and has held that position for twenty-eight years. He is assigned to Saint Michael's Military Parish, Fort Gordon, GA, and he has been the deacon there for twenty-nine years. He is a retired Army Medical Service Corps Officer as well as retired from the Medical College of Georgia, Augusta, GA.

Deacon Richard Halbur and his wife Yvonne are the parents of three children and the grandparents of eleven grandchildren. Deacon Richard ministers at St. Stephens First Martyr Catholic Church in Hinesville, GA, where he assists with Parish Youth Group and RCIA. Yvonne is a LPN, and Deacon Richard works with housing at Ft. Stewart, GA.

Deacon Dave Hayden and his wife Cathy are the parents of two sons, Patrick and Matthew. Deacon Dave is the Deacon at St. Michael's Catholic Church, Tybee Island, GA. He has been a teacher for eighteen years, and, currently, he is the Assistant Principal and the Director of Religious Education at St. Michael's Catholic School.

Deacon Bob Kepshire and his wife Cathy are the parents of two adult children. Deacon Bob is currently serving in both the Diocese of Savannah and the Archdiocese of Atlanta. He is the Chief Nursing Officer at Spalding Regional Medical Center/Tenet Health System Medical, Inc. in Griffin, GA.

Deacon Ken Maleck and his wife Patty are the parents of a son, Brian. Deacon Ken ministers at St. Mary's-on-the-Hill Catholic Church (Augusta, GA), where he is involved in adult faith formation ministries. He is a retired pharmaceutical chemist.

Deacon Michael McGrath and his wife Leticia are the parents of two sons, Matthew and Luke. Deacon Mike ministers to the Spanish-speaking and English-speaking communities at St. Matthew Catholic Church (Statesboro, GA). He is a professor of sixteenth- and seventeenth-century Spanish literature and culture at Georgia Southern University.

Deacon Patrick Mongan and his wife Ellen are the parents of eight children and seven grandchildren. After thirty years of teaching medical students and residents at the Medical College of Georgia, he retired from Family Practice to become a full time pastoral assistant at St. Joseph Catholic Church (Macon, GA).

Deacon Rey Morales and his wife Bessie live in Augusta, GA. Deacon Rey, a native of Puerto Rico, served in the U.S. Army for many years, and, currently, he is the Director of Hispanic Ministry for the Diocese of Savannah.

Deacon Bienvenido Perez, Jr. and his wife Pamela are the parents of three daughters: Jacqueline, Jennifer, and Angela. Deacon Ben ministers to a Military community at Our Lady Queen of Peace (Hunter AAF, GA). He is a Helicopter Standardization Instructor Pilot with the Department of Defense at Hunter Army Airfield in Savannah, Ga.

Deacon James Roberge and his wife Arlene have three children, Stephanie (Chris) Delcourt, James III and Julie, and two grandchildren, Brady and Kason Delcourt. A native of Bristol, CT, Air Force Academy graduate and AF civilian computer scientist, Deacon Jim ministers at St. Patrick Catholic Church in Perry, GA.

Deacon Joseph Soparas ministers at Saint Teresa of Avila Catholic Church in Grovetown, Georgia. He is a Physician Assistant at the Veterans Hospital in Augusta, Georgia. Deacon Joe and his wife

Mary have two daughters, Rebecca Edwards and Christina McTier. They have four grandchildren: Kalie, Justin, Gracie and Dalton.

Deacon Al Sullivan and his wife Debbie have two children, Jared (25) and Erin (23). Both Al & Debbie work for a hospital system in their home town of Augusta, GA., Al in the Finance Division and Debbie in Administration. Among other duties, Deacon Al administers Baptism preparation classes and the Children's Liturgy ministry for his parish.

Deacon Michael and Leticia McGrath
St. Matthew Catholic Church, Statesboro

Introduction

*A*NSWERING THE CALL IS the story of nineteen Catholic permanent deacons from the Diocese of Savannah (Georgia) whose lives underwent profound transformations as they embarked upon a journey of self-discovery which revealed to them both the awesome power of God and the holiness of everyday life. The deacons whose testimony you are about to read come from vastly different spiritual, professional and educational backgrounds; however, these differences became quite evident in the first diaconal formation class when each deacon revealed his life story and explained his wish to serve God. The common thread of these different, yet moving stories, was the beautiful way in which God was present in each of them. When these deacons responded to God's call, they soon became aware of the profound impact their decision would make on their lives as husbands, fathers, and, most of all, servants of God. While personal in nature, the testimony of each deacon is also universal in its scope. The changes each experienced is also the story of every person who opens his or her heart to God and allows Him to fashion it to His will.

The target audience of this book is by no means uniform. Any person who experiences a crisis of faith or wants to deepen his or her relationship with God, will find the theological, pastoral and spiritual aspects of these essays informative as they will inspire further reflection and discernment. Each of the essays can be read as a guide to ministry that provides personal and experiential advice about how to minister in a God-centered and healing manner. A person considering a religious vocation, or any man discerning God's call as a permanent deacon, or is a candidate or a deacon now, will appreciate the honesty with which each deacon describes the expected and unexpected stages of his journey.

The reader of the essays will soon discover that these deacons experienced at one time or another, the same feelings of doubt and unworthiness that many people feel when they examine their relationship with God. I ask that the reader keep in mind these two questions that the deacons asked themselves early in the formation program: "Why me?" and "Am I worthy?" Many people ask the same questions, whether they are considering religious life, service in some capacity to their church community, or perhaps undergoing a crisis of faith, wondering what God is calling them to do. The transformation that each deacon experienced began, for the most part, with the same two questions.

The author of the Preface of this book is Father Michael Cooper, S.J., a professor of theology at St. Leo University. In addition to being our spiritual director, Fr. Cooper served as the instructor during the first year of a five-year diaconal formation program, which included academic courses that satisfied the requirements of the Master of Arts degree in Pastoral Studies (St. Leo University).[1] The first year of the program focused upon the spiri-

---

1. The curriculum consisted of the following courses: Finding God in All Things: The Apostolic & World-Embracing Spirituality of Ignatius Loyola; CyberCulture in Pastoral Ministry, History of Christianity; Christian Spirituality; Christian Scriptures; Theological

tuality of St. Ignatius of Loyola, which became a catalyst for the personal and spiritual transformation that each deacon experienced. St. Ignatius' *Suscipe*, the Latin word for "Receive," in particular, resonated deeply:

> Take, Lord, and receive all my liberty, my memory, my understanding, and all my will—all that I have and possess. You, Lord, have given all that to me. I now give it back to you, O Lord. All of it is yours. Dispose of it according to your will. Give me love of yourself along with your grace, for that is enough for me.

A common theme of these essays is the many ways Ignatian spirituality can enrich the life of any person who seeks to balance a meaningful religious life with the demands of family and professional life.

Deacon George Foster, the Director of the Permanent Diaconate for the Diocese of Savannah, wrote the Epilogue of this book. The role of Deacon Foster and his wife Georgia in the journey of each of the deacons whose essay you are about to read is immeasurable. Their loving support, insightful guidance, and exemplary model of the "deacon couple" continue to be a source of inspiration and proof of the blessed life that awaits any person who serves God by sharing the Good News.

My brother deacons and I wish to express our gratitude to the following people who shaped our relationship with God in many ways through their actions and their words: Dr. Ty Anderson, Bishop Kevin Boland, James J. Caldwell and the volunteers from Immaculate Conception Catholic Church (Dublin, GA), Sr. Caroline Cerveny, Fr. Doug Clark, Fr. Michael Cooper, Fr. Daniel Firmin, Deacon George and Georgia Foster, Fr. Richard Hart, Dr. Robert Imperato, Fr. Anthony Kissel, Fr. Larry Madden, Fr. Jeremiah McCarthy, Dr. Paul Thigpen, Dr. Michael Tkacik, Dr. Pauline Viviano, and Fr. James Wallace. Finally, we dedicate this book to our families. The depth of our love and appreciation for their support cannot be expressed enough in words.

Deacon Michael McGrath
Statesboro, Georgia
August 23, 2009

Foundations; Hebrew Scriptures; Christian Ethics, World Religions; Worship, Liturgy, and Sacraments; Theology and Spirituality of Ministry.

Deacon J. Brian and Jill Bergeron
Our Divine Saviour Church, Tifton

J. Brian Bergeron

As ordination approached, I was reminded of the words of advice that my pastor Alfonso Gutiérrez shared with me: Enjoy the journey and do not worry about the final destination. I am so grateful for those words of wisdom. I can honestly say that I followed my friend's advice and the experience I have had since I answered God's call to serve Him has been the most wonderful journey of my life.

I can remember the first diaconal formation class in the quaint parish hall in Dublin, GA. Men of diverse backgrounds, traveling different paths, but all gathered for the same reason. Each and every one of us felt a call from God. Each and every one of us took the first step in answering His call; each and every one of us took a huge leap of faith. It has been my privilege to be a part of this Spirit-filled group of Catholic men, their wives and their families. It has been a journey I have shared with my wife Jill and my two precious daughters, Alexa and Abby. All three are truly God sent. Every time I think of them, I feel the true love of God. I consider myself the most blessed man on earth.

Answering God's call in my life, the dream He has for me, has always been an obsession of mine. I can recall one of our classes in which we participated in an exercise where we addressed our fears. My biggest fear has always been that I will not fulfill God's purpose in my life. I feel confident that this journey has opened my eyes to many things God is calling me to do. In sport's terms, the ball is now in my court. The time of discernment and preparation paved the way for me to play my small part in the building of God's Kingdom. The foundation has been laid; it is now my responsibility to build upon it.

It is obvious that each deacon in my class has been blessed with different and unique gifts. God encourages every one of us to embrace these gifts and to use them to praise and glorify Him. It didn't take long for me to realize that I had no calling (nor a desire) to become a theologian. My calling is not of the scholarly nature, and I am more than comfortable that my life will not go in that direction. My calling is one of evangelization, to spread the living Gospel. I began a ministry I named *Jesus Rocks Ministry* the first year of our formation. In this ministry, I challenge everyone to take an enthusiastic adventure into their faith, because it is what I do on a daily basis. I jump into my faith with a boundless enthusiasm, and this journey has given me even more encouragement to continue living my life in this way.

One of the most precious gifts that I now possess is the relationships I formed with my classmates and instructors. Deacon George Foster and his wife Georgia have answered their call. God is smiling on them as they manage this program in an efficient, loving and caring way. It would be impossible to count the number of lives this couple has touched, and their ministry is a testament to their love for God and their love for one another. Father Michael Cooper, my Jesuit companion, has touched my life in a very special way, and my family considers him family. He has been very supportive and instrumental in the early inception of my ministry, in particular with *Jesus Rocks Ministry*. He vested me at ordination. He is a blessing to my life and to my spirituality, which has always been rooted in the teaching of St. Ignatius. My father Ralph, my brother-in-law Phil, and I have made yearly retreats to the Manresa Jesuit retreat center in Convent, Louisiana for the last twenty-five years. It was at Manresa that I made my decision to enter the Diaconate program. It is a special place and God truly speaks to me there. I have also made friends and developed bonds with classmates that will never be broken. Six of us formed a group and met at a local restaurant after each Friday class for five years. The time we spent together, talking about grass-root ministry and our different ministries, was often as spiritually enlightening as any class. I feel strongly that the Diaconate is about ministering at the grass-root level. This type of ministry excites me, and I believe my deacon brothers share my sentiment.

I was not able to think about ordination without recalling my Catholic upbringing. I was fortunate to have a strong Catholic family. My maternal grandmother was the most Christ-like person I have ever met, and my parents have always been examples of God's love. In addition, my siblings and extended family have always been Catholic in the truest sense of the word.

It is very important to me that my parish knows how much I love them and how precious sharing this journey with them has been for me and Jill. My ordination was the result of a team effort. My heart overflows with love and gratitude for all who have been so supportive of me and my calling.

I am not certain where the Holy Spirit will lead me and my ministry. I am certain, however, that I now understand more than ever the importance of being open to the call. Looking back, the Lord has been calling; I just never picked up the phone. Now that I have, I understand the need to listen, to find God in the silence of my heart, as well as in the storm of everyday life.

My deacon brother Jerry Clark wrote me a note during a time when I was struggling, encouraging me to stay the course because God had given me the gifts to bring Jesus to other people. I still have that note and realize that God calls all of us to bring Jesus to others, with or without ordination. Each and every believer is called to be a witness to Christ. Each and every one of us has the responsibility to be a reflection of Jesus. Each and every one of us has a duty to answer our call.

I am excited that I have taken this step to answering God's call. It is my constant prayer that I live up to the responsibilities that come with my calling, and I hope that I never lose my enthusiasm for God's love for His people. I dream that the rest of my journey with Christ will be as enjoyable and rewarding as the first several years have been until now. May all I do always be for the greater glory of God so that my final destination be with Him in eternity.

Deacon John and Trish Blaha
St. Augustine Catholic Church, Thomasville

John Blaha

As I began my journey to becoming a deacon, I had no idea of what type of ministry I would become involved in when that day arrived. My only desire was to serve and help others with their own spiritual journeys. Having been blessed with a dedicated deacon in our parish for the past twenty years, his example gave me an idea of the different opportunities that would be available. At the beginning, I did not have a clear feeling for what my talents were, other than my life experiences, nor did I have a clear picture of what the ministry of a deacon was all about, other than assisting at Mass and helping with baptisms and other church-related duties, sacramental and non-sacramental.

God created each of us different from others. Everyone has a unique perspective as a result of his or her situation in life. It is a true blessing to be able to accept and to understand those differences: "The elitist person who denigrates human beings or classifies them in a hostile way, the promiscuous person who cannot live chastely, the insecure person who must either dominate others or flee from them-none of these are fit for ministry" (O'Meara 246).

We live in a fast-changing world. The expansion of knowledge and technology is moving at such a rapid pace, it is difficult to keep up with the changes. Likewise, these changes are happening in our parishes. The laity has different needs and desires. History shows us the Church has been slow to change in the past. Vatican II was a blessing and came just in time to open the doors to a new era. Even with the changes that have occurred, I wonder whether it is enough for today's youth or for the next generation. With the technology, especially iPODS and Blackberries, that today's teens are growing up with, what will their expectations be of the Church? Information available at the click of a few keys makes for an impatient society. Can we, as a Church, keep young people interested and active as Catholics since we are a Church that is big on tradition? Can we present Catholic theology to this generation in an effective and interesting way?

What can we do to attract and hold onto our young people? Will they do as I and many of my peers did, and return to the Church after a period of feeling that the Church is not necessary? My wife Trish and I realized the importance of raising our children in the Church. While my children do not attend Mass regularly, they grew into adults with principles. When and if the youth return to a church, will they return to the Catholic Church or will they choose one of the new mega non-denominational churches? What do we need to do to make the Catholic Church attractive to this new generation? How can I, as a deacon, help to make the Church attractive and relevant to the new technology-savvy generation? These are areas about which I am concerned, and I pray that my ministry will address the questions I have.

On the other end of the spectrum of the youth who evolve continually are a large percentage of people who cannot accept change. They want everything to remain as it was years ago, before Vatican II. In *Theology of Ministry*, Thomas O'Meara discusses this attitude, which he terms "antiquarianism." While there exists a common belief that history only encompasses the time from which a person is born, this attitude is problematic because it may restrict a person's view of the world to his or her lifetime. Clergy, in particular, should be open-minded in order to meet the people whom they minister to where they are in their lives. If we refuse to be flexible, the Church assumes the risk of becoming ineffective. If a parish becomes stagnated, it becomes difficult to attract new people to the Church. Not only will we not attract new converts, we will also have a difficult time retaining parishioners who grew up in the Church.

O'Meara notes that one of the main functions of the Catholic Church in the past was the education of children. The reason that the Church became a provider of education for children was the lack of an adequate public system that understood Catholic tradition. Adult education was not a primary concern. Even today, many parishes either do not offer adult education or do not do so as effectively as they should. The extent of adult education in many parishes is the priest's or deacon's homily at the Mass. Where there are programs for adults, only a small percentage of adults participate. Yes, we live in a busy and bursting-at-the-seams world, so how do we make this important aspect of Church life appealing to our parishioners? How do we instill the desire for adults to want to learn more about their faith and the Church? I ponder all of these questions and hope to answer them in my ministry.

"If in an unsettling way the dynamic parish of today resembles a Pauline community on A.D. 55 more than it resembles a parish in 1945" (34). This statement by O'Meara inspired in me many different thoughts about the Church and Christians, in general, today. We are in a battle for Christian ideals on many fronts, especially as society continues to become more secular with each passing day. I believe that the whole issue of state-supported religion, or separation of church and state, has been taken out of context. The proponents of a secular society are determined to succeed at any cost. They are an example of the need to remain steadfast, as those who make the most noise get heard. Christians have to become just as relentless and determined as the secularists. We have to engage ourselves in this attack upon our religious freedom.

Our Church and our faith have to be the focal point of our lives in order not to suppress all that Jesus gave His life to achieve. Our love for God and all that He has given us is vital to live a Christian life. We cannot live a monastic life, go into the desert and hope that everyone leaves us alone. We have to have the courage to be Christians and publicly display that we are Christians by how we live our lives. It is necessary for us to live a life that leaves no doubt in anyone's mind that we are Christians.

If a person knows more about the Church and understands that it is what Christ Himself ordained, this knowledge, in addition to learning more about the Catholic faith, will empower people, perhaps to the point where they can be proud to call themselves Catholics. Education is the key element, and we, both clergy and laity, must instill a desire in people to become more aware of what it is the Church believes and why. All of these issues become less of a problem when we are a well-educated and well-informed people.

According to O'Meara, "It is difficult to be a Catholic today without some education" (249). What can I do as a deacon to help fill this need for greater awareness of the faith? I have tried a couple of different approaches with some success. I have always felt and experienced that when you start a Bible study program, you attract only a small number of participants. So, I decided upon a different approach. I organized and facilitated a book study group. At first, it did attract more people than the number who attended the Bible study class, but the attendance, unfortunately, dropped off. The selection of the right book is one of the key factors to a successful experience. In spite of the waning attendance, I felt that the book study group was successful. Since I do not believe I am gifted with the ability to teach—I am more of an organizer—, I utilized this gift to set up the program. I selected a moderator to lead the class discussion. I was, in a way, testing the waters to see how successful of a program I could organize. The outcome was successful enough to try it again.

My next attempt at furthering adult education in my parish will be to lead discussions about Vatican II. I feel that there is little known about this period in the Church's history and its wide-reaching effects. Many people complain about the changes that we see every Sunday at Mass, but I believe it would be helpful to create an opportunity for people to learn more about the changes and the Church's history. Ignorance is dangerous and costly. Without knowledge, we wander without any real direction or purpose. The many areas that have been opened to the laity are one very important aspect of the Church that should be of interest to all. Vatican II changed the laity's role from passive to active. Lectors and Extraordinary Ministers of the Eucharist are only two important ministries in which the laity can take part. These ministries, among other opportunities to become involved in church life, provide parishioners, both male and female, with the opportunity to become more involved in the Mass and the life of the Church.

My ministry as a deacon fulfills a desire in me that started more than twenty years ago, when I first began to hear God's call. Over the years, I found many reasons why I should not answer God's call. At first, I did not see ministry as a calling from God, but, rather, it was just something that I would like to do. I did not understand that it was God who instilled that desire in me, His way of calling. It has taken prayer and discernment for me to understand that it is what God wants of me, and not just something I want. He wants me to give of myself, to give and share the experiences and the knowledge that I have acquired in life. My life will be the basis upon which I draw strength in ministry.

I feel called to an area such as marriage preparation, particularly preparing people who are considering entering into a second marriage. As a result of my own experience, I know the challenges and problems that can arise when two families become one. I feel empowered to give guidance to children of blended families before they experience any problems that might arise. Adult children can be just as much of a challenge as children still living at home. They present a different set of challenges.

As I began to read the last chapter of O'Meara's book, the author addressed some of my questions and concerns. In his short paragraph on "Discernment" (239), numerous statements enlightened and comforted me. A good ministry begins with openness to people without letting the changes and struggles of life stand in your way. Life presents different challenges to each person. The sins and failures can not be a deterrent or an obstacle in being able to minister to someone. Openness is the main ingredient. It is absolutely necessary to remain non-judgmental with respect to our own biases. After all, we did not live the life of the person to whom we minister. We have to learn, according to O'Meara, to be a prophet or apostle instead of an entrepreneur. Since I have always considered myself an entrepreneur, this idea caught my attention. I interpret it to mean that we should follow the pattern and lessons that Jesus taught his apostles. We should not think that we are smarter than Jesus by trying to come up with better or more effective methods. We should not try to be an entrepreneur by "reinventing the wheel" of saving souls. We have the ultimate example to follow.

Jesus rejected all honors His followers tried to bestow upon Him. Jesus came to serve and not to rule, and He was dedicated to the mission His father sent him to do, and serve God was all that Jesus wanted to do: "The opposite of service is ambition for display and power" (O'Meara 242). This statement is a profound one. When we center our lives upon financial success and material goods, we are no longer the servants that God wants us to be. When I answered God's call, the goals I had set for material goods had a new meaning. Goals and ambition to be a good servant are necessary, but the end result must be different. As a servant of God, the attainment of a goal is not for personal gratification, but it is to help others reach their goals of living a good Christian life. If my work is done for my gratification, then I am a failure; it is done for the wrong reason. This lesson is the same one that I was taught in sales training. My objective was to help people gain or buy what they need to improve their lives. If a salesman or a saleswoman makes a sale only to receive a commission without focusing upon the benefit of the customer, he or she has committed sales malpractice.

In my ministry, any accomplishments I experience must be kept private, as I do not aspire to hang a plaque next to the "Salesman of Year" that reads "Saver of Souls of The Year." Honor and reward will be the knowledge that an attempt was made to help someone. I have to keep Jesus as my example by living my life as Jesus would have me do. This goal may be a high one, but it will help me to focus on the mission of my calling and lead me on the path to success.

I have been blessed with many talents and skills. I consider myself "a jack of many trades but master of none," and this philosophy guides my ministry. I can draw from my life's experiences because they have been many and diversified. I pray that what I have learned throughout my life will help me to be the best servant of God I can be as I serve Him and the Church as a permanent deacon.

My journey to becoming a deacon was a long one. It started in the spring of 1982 when I attended a *Cursillo* weekend. It was there that I learned of God's unconditional love for me and that God accepted us as we are. Commit yourself to follow Jesus and nothing else matters. I met several holy men who had made commitments to being good Catholics; several were already deacons and others became deacons. These men made lasting impressions on me, and it was at this point in my life that I heard God's call. I knew then service to God was something that I could and should do.

Shortly after that weekend, I lost my wife to a tragic suicide. Due to spending the next ten years as a single parent, raising my children and getting my life in order, the calling to become a deacon laid dormant. I would occasionally give thought to the possibility, but I always came up with reasons why I should not pursue this path. The time was not right. When I learned about another formation class, there was no hesitation or questions. I knew that the time was right for me to answer God's call, so I started the application process. The journey has been long, it has been fun, and it has been a great deal of hard work. The rewards will be greater than the hardships, though.

Today, I know that my ministry as a deacon is the work of God; I am following God's call. The effectiveness of my ministry will be judged by history. I have expressed my concerns for our Church and its people. Now, the time has come to continue addressing the issues I have brought up in this essay. How I will live out my mission is in God's hands. My calling is to listen to God and do as I am led. At times, it will be difficult. I know that at times the work will be frustrating and thankless. Any challenges I face cannot become a deterrent as I seek to serve God. I know He will be standing beside me, guiding me, at all times in my life. I am ready and eager to serve Him.

BIBLIOGRAPHY

O' Meara, Thomas F., O.P. *Theology of Ministry*. Mahwah, NJ: Paulist Press, 1999.

Deacon Tirso and Annette Castillo
Immaculate Conception Catholic Church, Dublin

Tirso A. Castillo

BEFORE ENTERING THE DIACONATE program for the Diocese of Savannah, I was a spiritual poodle on a leash. I knew lots of rules; for example, one must fast one hour before Mass. After having completed the five years of the diaconate formation program, I now consider myself an Australian sheep dog on no leash. In other words, I feel that I have been transformed from a servant capable only of slavishly adhering to a code of rules into a loving servant that can think independently in matters of faith and ministry.

Many contributed to this transformation, but one person clearly stands out. With his love of Jesus and his infectious enthusiasm for ministry, Father Michael Cooper, S.J. helped me go from being a spiritual child to a spiritual adult. Father Michael was the one who taught me that it was more important to be present for someone in need (contemplative in action) than it was whether the person had fasted one hour before Mass or not.

The other dominant force in my transformation was the company of my brothers of the diaconate class. Often, my dear wife and I will reminisce about the privilege and joy of sharing the diaconate formation process with such a company of exceptional individuals. Repeatedly, their collected wisdom served as a source of personal enrichment for me.

What follows are my reflections on a number of issues pertaining to ministry written just prior to my ordination. These thoughts are not intended to be a formal theological presentation, but they are representative of my transformation as a result of my diaconate formation journey.

On October 28, 2007, Pope Benedict XVI beatified 498 Christian martyrs of the Spanish Civil War (1936–1939). Among this group were two bishops, 24 diocesan priests, 462 members of religious orders, one seminarian, one deacon, one subdeacon, and seven laypersons. During the Spanish communist persecution of this period, over 9,000 people died as martyrs for their Christian faith.

I am inspired by and deeply identify with one of these martyrs, Brother José López Piteira. His parents, Emilio and Lucinda, were both from the northern region of Spain (Galicia) and emigrated to Cuba in 1909. They settled in the town of Arroyo Blanco of Camaguey Province. Br. José was born on March 27, 1913 and was baptized on November 11 of the same year. At age 5, his parents returned to Spain and established a family home in the northern town of Partovia. Few details are known of the early life of Br. José. It is known that by age 14, however, he was a student at the Benedictine monastery of Santa Maria de San Clodio. His novitiate and first religious vows were made at the Augustinian convent of our Lady of Good Counsel of Laganes at age 20 on August 20, 1929.

Br. José subsequently entered the Benedictine monastery of El Escorial (Madrid). Here, he completed his studies in philosophy and theology. Br. José made his permanent religious vows on July 16, 1934. He was ordained a subdeacon on April 6, 1935 by Bishop Leopoldo Eijo Garay of Madrid, and a deacon on September 8, 1935, the feast day of the patroness of Cuba,

Our Lady of Charity. It is not known whether this date was selected on purpose or by coincidence. What is known is that Br. José remained proud all of his life of being born in Cuba and being a Cuban citizen.

The terrible Communist-led persecutions against Christians began in 1931. The Communist commissar of Madrid, Santiago Carrillo, personally gave orders for the execution of over 3,000 priests, nuns and other religious. On August 6, 1936 El Escorial monastery was stormed by Communist troops, and Br. José, along with all the other religious present, was arrested. They were detained at San Anton prison (Madrid) in harsh and cruel conditions. Countless appeals for assistance were made by the López Piteira family to the Cuban diplomatic representatives in Spain. After considerable effort, the Cuban consular officials managed to obtain permission from the Spanish Communist authorities for Br. José's release based on his Cuban citizenship.

When informed of his option to leave the prison and spare his life, Deacon José López Piteira responded, "Here is where all of you who have been my educators, my teachers, my superiors are. What shall I do in the city? I prefer to share the same lot as the rest, may it be what God wills" (Fernández González). No one would have criticized him had he resorted to using his Cuban citizenship to save his own life.

On November 30, 1936 Br. José and fifty other Augustinian religious were stripped of all possessions. Their hands were bound, and they were placed on buses to Paracuello de Jarama, a terrible place of execution. While they were on the buses, the religious prayed for the forgiveness of their executioners. Br. José's final words were, "Viva Cristo Rey" ("Long live Christ the King"). He was twenty-four years old at the time of his execution. It was reported that the courageous Christian witness of Br. José and the other Augustinians was so powerful that even the executioners were left in awe.

Br. José's life exemplified Christian love. Especially notable was Br. José's love for Jesus, love for his religious vocation, and love for the members of his religious community. It would not be a stretch to say even love for his executioners. Given the love that I have experienced during my own formation experience towards the diaconate, I can deeply understand Br. José's reluctance to leave his brothers and professors.

Love is the core essence of my own ministry; that is, my relationship with God and the actions of my life: "Whoever is without love does not know God, for God is love" (1 John 4:8). God's call for us to love can be traced to the earliest passages of Judeo-Christian salvation history: "Love your neighbor as yourself. I am the Lord" (Lev 19:18).

Love is the root of the great Commandments. "Teacher, which commandment in the law is the greatest?" He said to him, "You shall love the Lord, your God, with all your heart, with all your soul, and with all your mind." This one is the greatest and the first Commandment. The second Commandment is like it: "You shall love your neighbor as yourself. The whole law and the prophets depend on these two commandments" (Matt 22:36–40). The Gospels of Mark and Luke present very similar passages (Mark 12:29–31; Luke 10:26–27). Perhaps even more pertinent to those in ministry, "I give you a new commandment: love one another. As I have loved you, so you also should love one another" (John 13:34).

Jesus, however, exhorts us to go beyond common human conventions and to reach for an extreme degree of love: "But to you who hear I say, love your enemies, do good to those who hate you, bless those who curse you, pray for those who mistreat you" (Luke 6:27–28). This call to "love your enemies" can also be found in the Gospel of Matthew (5:44).

Love at its most radical expression is Eucharistic love: "This is my commandment: love one another as I love you. No one has greater love than this, to lay down one's life for one's friends" (John 15:12–13). In the setting of Eucharistic love, personal egoisms disappear as each individual generously gives of himself for the well-being of other persons. St. Paul reminds us that this is what Jesus did for us on the cross: "Christ loved the church and handed himself over for her" (Eph 5:25).

For Jesus, love is more than an abstraction. Love becomes a link to the incarnational: "Jesus answered and said to him, 'Whoever loves me will keep my word, and my father will love him, and we will come to him and make our dwelling with him'" (John 14:23). In the post-Resurrection exchange between Simon Peter and Our Lord, Jesus is very explicit that love for Him is joined to service for others (ministry): "Jesus said to Simon Peter, 'Simon, son of John, do you love me more than these?' [. . .] 'Feed my sheep'" (John 21:15–17). St. Paul makes the point that to be incarnational means to remain rooted in the love of Jesus Christ: "For in Christ Jesus, neither circumcision nor uncircumcision counts for anything but only faith expressing itself through love" (Gal 5:6). Love is what enables the individual to answer the call to ministry in the affirmative: "It was not you who chose me, but I who chose you and appointed you to go and bear fruit that will remain, so that whatever you ask the Father in my name he may give to you" (John 15:16).

Adapting Thomas O'Meara's model of concentric circles to the process of describing my own ministry, love can be described as being the core circle. Surrounding the core circle, and not necessarily in a concentric manner, would be other aspects of ministry such as teaching, preaching and healing. These, of course, are not the only activities of ministry, but they appear to have been dominant in the public life and ministry of Our Lord: "He went around all of Galilee, teaching in their synagogues, proclaiming the gospel of the kingdom, and curing every disease and illness among the people" (Matt 4:23).

It should not be much of a surprise that the "Word became flesh" (John 1:14) should assume a prominent teaching role. Throughout the four Gospels Jesus is referred to as teacher (Matt 8:19; Matt 19:16; Mark 4:38; Mark 9:17; Mark 10:20; Luke 3:12; Luke 11:45; John 1:38; John 8:4). Jesus never refers to himself as priest, but he does refer to himself as Teacher (Matt 26:18; Mark 14:14; Luke 22:11; John 13:13). Similarly, Mary does not refer to Jesus as priest but as " 'Rabbouni,' which means Teacher" (John 20:16).

The following passage from the Gospel of Matthew especially resonates in my current and future ministry: "Therefore, whoever breaks one of the least of these commandments and teaches others to do so will be called least in the kingdom of heaven. But whoever obeys and teaches these commandments will be called greatest in the kingdom of heaven" (Matt 5:19). During the past six years, I have been responsible for the Rite of Christian Initiation of Adults (RCIA) program at Immaculate Conception Church (Dublin, GA). It is my hope to develop a diocesan-wide program for the RCIA someday. Undoubtedly, this program would be multimedia, most likely a PowerPoint-based program. Along similar lines, I would like to see a program of adult catechesis developed. No less important, I would like to remain active in the future formation and education of deacons. I find this work to be intellectually and spiritually exciting (life-giving).

Equally as important as teaching in the ministry of our Lord was preaching: "He told them, 'Let us go on to the nearby villages that I may preach there also. For this purpose have I come.' So he went into their synagogues, preaching and driving out demons throughout the whole of Galilee" (Mark 1:38–39). Jesus unambiguously commissioned the disciples:

"Go into the whole world and proclaim the gospel to every creature" (Mark 16:15). This ministry also has special pertinence to me given that in our rural community of central Georgia there are very few people who can preach the Gospels to the many Hispanics who do not understand English.

Few experiences are as universal as the absence of health: "His fame spread to all of Syria, and they brought to him all who were sick with various diseases and racked with pain, those who were possessed, lunatics, and paralytics and he cured them" (Matt 4:24). Without exception, every culture knows firsthand the morbid impact caused by the lack of physical, mental or spiritual soundness. The miracles of healing were perhaps the most dramatic in the public life of Jesus, because every human person can connect with the notion of health restored: "He took the child by the hand and said to her, 'Talitha koum,' which means, 'Little girl, I say to you, arise!' " (Mark 5:41).

Healing was so important to Jesus' ministry that he extended this power to his disciples: "He summoned the Twelve and gave them power and authority over all demons and to cure disease, and he sent them to proclaim the kingdom of God and to heal [the sick]" (Luke 9:1–2). As modern ministers, it is critical that we keep present that ministering is not a business of judgment but a business of healing. Our efforts at helping others heal need to remain deeply rooted in God's love for us and our love for God. Jesus declared that he had the power to heal the body, but more importantly the soul as well: "Which is easier, to say to the paralytic, 'Your sins are forgiven,' or to say, 'Rise, pick up your mat and walk' " (Mark 2:9)? As a physician of nearly twenty-three years, I can attest that often the etiology of physical illness is spiritual illness. Data presented at a symposium of the American College of Gastroenterology revealed that at least 25% of all women with chronic abdominal pain and irritable bowel syndrome had been sexually abused as children. The data also showed that until these patients worked through their guilt and shame, physical recovery was unlikely.

Very importantly, Jesus taught that infirmity was not a reflection of moral/spiritual corruption: "As he passed by he saw a man blind from birth. His disciples asked him, 'Rabbi who sinned this man or his parents, that he was born blind?' Jesus answered, 'Neither he nor his parents sinned; it is so that the works of God might be made visible through him' " (John 9:1–3).

The hemorrhagic woman's encounter with Our Lord illustrates that in ministry healing is a two way process: "Immediately her flow of blood dried up. She felt in her body that she was healed of her affliction" (Mark 5:29). The recipient's faith is a vital component to the efficacy of the work of the minister. Furthermore, "So he was not able to perform any mighty deed (miracle) there, apart from curing a few sick people by laying his hands on them" (Mark 6:5). Time and time again I have observed patients sabotage their recovery through their failure to join a therapeutic alliance with their physician. Faced with a situation that lacks a reasonable therapeutic alliance, the ministering person should not be reluctant to bring this relationship to a close. Every ministering person has the professional privilege to seek consultation when dealing with difficult situations. Failure to terminate a pathologic ministering relationship can lead to an unhealthy situation of burnout and death dealing for the minister.

Several years ago, I was asked to see a patient who had far advanced end-stage cholangiocarcinoma. Her death was imminent from bile duct obstruction and liver failure. The patient had (has) a wonderful positive attitude, and I was able to successfully place a metal biliary stent into her left hepatic duct. This device gave her immediate biliary drainage. Her condition quickly improved and before going home I gave her my copy of Bernie Siegel's book, *Love, Medicine and Miracles: Lessons Learned about Self-Healing from a Surgeon's Experience with Exceptional Patience*. I was not sure if she would live long enough to read it. She subsequently went on to take a full dose of chemotherapy, however, and by all measures the patient's course has been remarkable. She is not cured of her cancer, but she has not succumbed to it either. She leads a full and rich life with her husband, children and grandchildren.

At this point, I would like to venture further out into the periphery of my adaptation of O'Meara's concentric circle model for describing ministry. As I have noted above, as I progress towards the periphery, my circles are not necessarily concentric—I would like to emphasize that when it comes to ministry one topic is not necessarily more important than another topic. In what follows, I would like to consider the meaning of being a contemplative in action, the importance of baptism, social justice, treatment of immigrants, the role of women in ministry, servant leadership and the deacon manager.

Ministry by necessity is incarnational: "Religion that is pure and undefiled before God and the Father is this: to care for orphans and widows in their affliction and to keep oneself unstained by the world" (Jas 1:27). Before we can minister to the person's mind and soul we have to minister to their stomach: "If a brother or sister has nothing to wear and has no food for the day, and one of you says to them, 'Go in peace, keep warm, and eat well,' but you do not give them the necessities of the body, what good is it? So also faith of itself, if it does not have works, is dead" (Jas 2:15–17). This notion is repeated in a separate analogy: "For just as a body without a spirit is dead, so also faith without works is dead" (Jas 2:26).

The union between the spiritual and the incarnational is perhaps best exemplified by St. Ignatius of Loyola, who, according to De Guibert, lived a life of service: "His mysticism was not confined to loving union with God in prayer but was oriented toward execution and loving service" (qtd. in De Guibert). The minister acting as a contemplative in action is able to preserve a connection between the spiritual and the incarnational.

The fact that Our Lord submitted himself to a baptism that he did not need underscores the importance of baptism in the life of a Christian: "Then Jesus came from Galilee to John at the Jordan to be baptized by him. John tried to prevent him, saying, 'I need to be baptized by you, and yet you are coming to me?' Jesus said to him in reply, 'Allow it now, for thus it is fitting for us to fulfill all righteousness' " (Matt 3:13–16). Jesus unambiguously asserted the necessity of faith and baptism for salvation: "Whoever believes and is baptized will be saved; whoever does not believe will be condemned" (Mark 16:16). Equally as explicit is the following passage: "Jesus answered, 'Amen, amen, I say to you, no one can enter the kingdom of God without being born of water and Spirit' " (John 3:5). Our Lord mandated universal baptism: "Go therefore, and make disciples of all nations, baptizing them in the name of the Father, and of the Son, and of the Holy Spirit" (Matt 28:19).

In *Pneumatic Correctives*, Thomas McGonigle and Michael Tkacik present the concept that at the time of baptism the Christian is baptized priest, prophet and king. By virtue of their Christian dignity, the baptized are privileged with full participation in the life of the Church: "But you are 'a chosen race, a royal priesthood, a holy nation, a people of his own, so that you may announce the praises' of him who called you out of darkness into his wonderful light" (1 Pet 2:9). Father Thomas O'Meara, in his book *Theology of Ministry*, expresses the same concept, but he expresses it in terms of claiming one's diaconal ministry. Father O'Meara further expands: "As sacramental initiation bestows new life and confirms faith, baptism also initiates a person into charism and diaconal action, into a community that is essentially ministerial" (211).

Our baptismal dignity is not only important for full participation in the Church, but it serves as the basis for claiming our giftedness. By recognizing our divinely endowed gifts, we are in turn empowered to maximize the fruits of our unique ministries. Our Lord was very clear that we are not only expected to claim our gifts but to develop them more fully: "I tell you, to everyone who has, more will be given, but from the one who has not, even what he has will be taken away" (Luke 19:26).

Helping others claim their giftedness ultimately means helping them to be empowered. The traditional paradigm that we believe something or do something because we are told to do so is an impediment to the empowerment of the Christian faithful. As deacon ministers we need to help our Christian sisters and brothers become spiritual adults through education, inspiration, service and prayer. Being a spiritual adult does not mean loving Jesus or his Church any less. Being a spiritual adult means making the most of the one's giftedness on behalf of the kingdom of God.

Proportionately, Americans spend less of their income on food than any other people on Earth. In part, this is due to the unequaled efficiency, ingenuity and industry of the American farmer. It is also due to the plentiful cheap labor available from Latin America. Supermarkets in the United States are filled with inexpensive fruits and vegetables while migrant farm workers live in deplorable conditions, many directly out of their cars (personal observation while working in a migrant farm worker health clinic, Ft. Pierce, FL). Other sectors of our economy such as construction, landscape maintenance, the restaurant industry and domestic service thrive given the availability of desperate workers from Latin America who are looking to improve conditions for themselves and their families.

As Catholics who celebrate the Eucharist each Sunday, we offend God if we are oblivious to the plight of our brothers and sisters around the world. "What care I for the number of your sacrifices? says the LORD. I have had enough of whole-burnt rams and fat of fatlings; In the blood of calves, lambs and goats I find no pleasure. When you come in to visit me, who asks these things of you? Trample my courts no more! Bring no more worthless offerings; your incense is loathsome to me. New moon and sabbath, calling of assemblies, octaves with wickedness: these I cannot bear. Your new moons and festivals I detest; they weigh me down, I tire of the load" (Isa 1:11–14).

God is not interested in hollow pretentious liturgies: "When you spread out your hands, I close my eyes to you; though you pray the more, I will not listen. Your hands are full of blood!" (Isa 1:15). What God really desires is moral conduct, kindness and social justice: "Wash yourselves clean! Put away your misdeeds from before my eyes; cease doing evil; learn to do good. Make justice your aim: redress the wronged, hear the orphan's plea, defend the widow" (Isa 1:16–17). Jesus taught that what is important is how we treat each other and not religious rituals: "Go and learn the meaning of the words, 'I desire mercy, not sacrifice'" (Matt 9:13).

The Old Testament teaches that in addition to being just, we need to be charitable: "Likewise, you shall not pick your vineyard bare, nor gather up the grapes that have fallen. These things you shall leave for the poor and the alien. I, the Lord, am your God" (Lev 19:10). God requires not just accidental charity, but an active intent to be charitable. "When you reap the harvest of your land, you shall not be so thorough that you reap the field to its very edge, nor shall you glean the stray ears of your grain. These things you shall leave for the poor and the alien. I, the Lord, am your God" (Lev 23:22). As noted above, Jesus links devotion to Him with incarnational charity: "For I was hungry and you gave me food, I was thirsty and you gave me drink, a stranger and you welcomed me, naked and you clothed me, ill and you cared for me, in prison and you visited me" (Matt 25:35–36).

The phenomenon of human migration is as ancient as society itself. Mankind resorts to movement in order to alleviate political, social and economic deprivation. The social calamity of human migration has been and continues to be a blight for all humanity. The tragedy often does not end at the border. Once the individual crosses the border, issues of family separation, social corruption and labor exploitation come into play.

The Old Testament teaches that the Jewish nation once existed in a foreign land. During their exile, the Hebrews were subjected to harsh and inhumane treatment. Having lived through this experience, divine justice would not allow for the Hebrews to perpetuate this evil on others: "You shall not oppress an alien; you well know how it feels to be an alien, since you were once aliens yourselves in the land of Egypt" (Exod 23:9). Humane treatment of immigrants is not only a matter of historical justice, but also a requirement of God: "You shall treat the alien who resides with you no differently that the natives born among you; have the same love for him as for yourself; for you too were once aliens in the land of Egypt. I, the Lord, am your God" (Lev 19:34). In fact, this passage raises the level of our moral responsibility. We are not only to treat immigrants fairly, we are to have "love for him as for yourself."

Moses taught that justice should be applied fairly even to the alien: "I charged your judges at that time, Listen to complaints among your kinsmen, and administer true justice to both parties even if one of them is an alien" (Deut 1:16). The immigrant should not only benefit from the same laws, but in a broader sense, from justice itself. In fact, to deny justice to an immigrant is to invoke the wrath of God: "Cursed be he who violates the rights of the alien, the orphan or the widow" (Deut 27:19)! Even in cases involving the death of a person, the Old Testament dictated that justice is not to be denied an immigrant: "These were the designated cities to which any Israelite or stranger living among them who had killed a person accidentally might flee to escape death at the hand of the avenger of blood, until he could appear before the community" (Josh 20:9).

The process of social assimilation is also described in the Jewish Scriptures: "You shall allot it as inheritances for yourselves and for the aliens resident in your midst who have bred children among you. The latter shall be to you like native Israelites; along with you they shall receive inheritances among the tribes of Israel" (Ezek 47:22). This social mandate seems to originate directly from God: "In whatever tribe the alien may be resident, there you shall assign him his inheritance, says the Lord God" (Ezek 47:23).

The Old Testament prohibits exploiting immigrants as cheap labor: "You shall not defraud a poor and needy hired servant, whether he be one of your own countrymen or one of the aliens who live in your communities" (Deut 24:14). The preceding instruction on social justice can best be summarized with the following words: "Thus says the Lord: Do what is right and just. Rescue the victim from the hand of his oppressor. Do not wrong or oppress the resident alien, the orphan, or the widow" (Jer 22:3).

From the first moments of Jesus' ministry, women have played an important and indispensable role in the church: "Accompanying him [...] Joanna, the wife of Herod's steward Chuza, Susanna, and many others who provided for them out of their resources" (Luke 8:3). Often, I feel that women are spiritually more advanced than men: "While he was still seated on the bench, his wife sent him a message, 'Have nothing to do with that righteous man. I suffered much in a dream today because of him'" (Matt 27:19). How many men have reached positions of prominence with the aid of prayers from loving and pious grandmothers, mothers, sisters, wives and daughters?

At the lowest point in our Church's history, when Jesus was arrested, tried and crucified, all the "macho" men abandoned Our Lord: "And they all left to him and fled" (Mark 14:50). The Disciples not only left Jesus unaided, but they would not even admit to knowing Him: "But he denied it saying, 'Woman, I do not know him' " (Luke 22:57). While Our Lord carried his cross, it was the women that were present: "A large crowd of people followed Jesus, including many women who mourned and lamented him" (Luke 23:27). Where were the Disciples when Jesus needed help carrying his cross? "As they led him away they took hold of a certain Simon, a Cyrenian, who was coming in from the country; and after laying the cross on him, they made him carry it behind Jesus" (Luke 23:26).

The women witnessed the Crucifixion: "There were also women looking on from a distance. Among them were Mary Magdalene, Mary, the mother of the younger James and of Joses, and Salome. These women had followed him when he was in Galilee and ministered to him. There were also many other women who had come up with him to Jerusalem" (Mark 15:40–41). It was the women who were first privileged to know about the Resurrection: "Then the angel said to the women in reply, 'Do not be afraid! I know that you are seeking Jesus the crucified. He is not here, for he has been raised just as he said. Come and see the place where he lay'" (Matt 28:5–6).

Women were present in the life of the primitive Church: "All these devoted themselves with one accord to prayer, together with some women, and Mary the mother of Jesus, and his brothers" (Acts 1:14). In addition, women were important early converts to Christianity: "One of them, a woman named Lydia, a dealer in purple cloth, from the city of Thyatira, a worshiper of God, listen, and the Lord opened her heart to pay attention to what Paul was saying" (Acts 16:14). It appears that women were so important to the early success of the Church that Paul repeatedly makes reference to them: "Some of them were convinced and joined Paul and Silas; so, too, a great number of Greeks who were worshippers and not a few of the prominent women" (Acts 17:4).

How can it be then, if women were so instrumental to the success of the early Church, that they can be denied full participation in the institutional Church? In some dioceses, girls are not allowed to function as altar servers and women are not allowed to have their feet washed during

Easter Tridiuum services! Pope John Paul II observed, "There is no doubt that the equal dignity and responsibility of men and women fully justifies women's access to public functions" (*Familiaris Consortio* #23). John Paul II further elaborated, "With due respect to the different vocations of men and women, the Church must in her own life promote as far as possible their equality of rights and dignity: and this for the good of all, the family, the Church and society" (*Familiaris Consortio* #23).

The unfortunate trend towards clericalism has led to a form of leadership that has not been in keeping with the model of servant leadership that Jesus taught: "But Jesus summoned them and said, 'You know that the rulers of the Gentiles lord it over them, and the great ones make their authority over them felt. But it shall not be so among you. Rather, whoever wishes to be great among you shall be your servant; whoever wishes to be first among you shall be your slave' " (Matt 20:25–27). In a remarkable display of humility, Jesus reinforces the importance of servant leadership: "If I, therefore, the master and teacher, have washed your feet, you ought to wash one another's feet" (John 13:14). A token reversal of this trend came with the election of Pope John Paul I (Albino Luciani), who was the first modern pope to decline the *sedia gestatoria* (ambulatory throne) and the papal tiara. His successors, Pope John Paul II and Pope Benedict XVI, have also declined such ostentatious symbols.

As servant leaders, we need to remain ever mindful that, "Whoever exalts himself will be humbled; but whoever humbled himself will be exalted" (Matt 23:12). Humility does not mean a false humility or a pathologic humility that prevents the minister from claiming God's given individual giftedness: "As each one has received a gift, use it to serve one another as good stewards of God's varied grace" (1 Pet 4:10). It does mean that we have a healthy claim to our gifts for the purposes of serving the kingdom of God and not for self-aggrandizement.

It is unfortunate for some individuals that ministry becomes the means to satisfy a desperate psychological need for self-recognition: "All their works are performed to be seen. They widen their phylacteries and lengthen their tassels. They love places of honor at banquets, seats of honor in synagogues, greetings and marketplaces, and the salutation 'Rabbi' " (Matt 23:5–7). Obviously, this attitude is not compatible with servant leadership. To some degree, we all like to be recognized. Ministry is not served well, however, when the individual minister is driven by narcissistic tendencies.

Being a good manager may not be as lofty an attribute as philanthropic service, but it is just as indispensable to the success of ministry. Good management skills require a strong sense of balance: "Deacons may be married only once and must manage their children and their households well" (1 Tim 3:12). Insufficient balance is a recipe for ministry burnout.

I have always been struck with how different the apostles were as men. Listening to the collective wisdom of my brothers in the diaconate formation, I can appreciate the same thing. I have come to realize what a blessing these differences are. We each reflect unique giftedness and weaknesses. What is important is that we support each other in our weaknesses and grow from each other's wisdom.

It is important to remember that each person is uniquely gifted, and it is not possible to be super minister doing every ministerial task with perfection. Just because one is not good at youth ministry does not mean that one is a failure. Unrealistic ministry expectations are unhealthy and will eventually result in ministry burnout. My brothers in the diaconate formation have blessed me with their wisdom and have helped me accept my own weaknesses and to be at peace with my limitations.

Standing at the periphery of my adaptation of O'Meara's concentric circle model for describing ministry, I can see a servant leader working with female colleagues, delivering diaconal services (a contemplative in action) such as teaching, preaching, healing and baptizing, but always rooted in a core of love: "Whoever preaches, let it be with the words of God; whoever serves, let it be with the strength that God supplies, so that in all things God may be glorified through Jesus Christ, to whom belong glory and dominion forever and ever. Amen" (1 Pet 4:11). ¡Viva Cristo Rey!

BIBLIOGRAPHY

De Guibert, Joseph. *The Jesuits: Their Spiritual Doctrine and Practice*. 3rd ed. Translated byW.J. Young. St. Louis, MO: Institute of Jesuit Sources, 1986.

Fernández González, Miguel Ángel. "El primer beato cubano, fray José López Piteira." Zenit (2007) n.pag. Online. Internet. 28 Oct. 2007.

McGonigle, Thomas C. and Michael Tkacik. *Pneumatic Correctives: What is the Spirit Sayingto the Church of the 21st Century?* Lanham, MD: University Press of America, 2006.

O' Meara, Thomas F., O. P. *Theology of Ministry*. Mahwah, NJ: Paulist Press, 1999.

Deacon Jerry and Judy Clark
St. Frances Cabrini Catholic Church, Savannah

Jerry Clark

MINISTRY IS A CALLING—a calling from God to serve. No one can bestow grace on themselves or give themselves charisms for ministry; they must come from the Holy Spirit, i.e., ministers are empowered by the Holy Spirit through God's Grace: "Ministry serves the divine life itself—and a human being cannot control or create grace" (O'Meara 227).

During the five-year diaconate formation program, our diaconate class experienced a multitude of instructors. The most effective ones were those who not only had the knowledge but a passion for their subject. They believed what they were teaching; it was obvious in the delivery and enthusiasm for their subject matter. The passion and energy in their message and its delivery were as important as the message itself. It is important that your message comes from who you are—your heart as well as your head.

The same is true for those involved in ministry, be they ordained, religious, or lay people. Those people with a passion for the Lord, and those filled with the Holy Spirit are the most effective, i.e., they became what they believed—ministers for the Lord. With Spirit filled people, the aura of the Spirit exudes from their being—their actions and words; the deep-felt passion for the subject makes it more credible and interesting, i.e., you listen with a keener interest, taking more away from the discussion or contributing with greater enthusiasm and vigor by assisting or participating in the ministry.

Ministry is relationships—relationships in the service of God, with the Holy Spirit, with community, with family and supporters, and with self. The foundation of any relationship is knowledge of who you are, your values, your desires, and your ambitions—a complete, objective analysis of self. Effective ministry requires knowledge of self, knowing your strengths as well as your limitations, and then acting on this knowledge: "In an incarnational faith, ministry exists at the intersection of the human and the divine, at the invisible horizon where grace seeks to become concrete in word, celebration, and person" (O'Meara 229).

The greatest difference between the person I am today versus when I began the formation process centers on my prayer life and faith maturity. I was very immature in my faith. I did not think so at the time but now realize that I had not done this self-analysis—at least objectively. I did not know my strengths nor admit to my weaknesses, and I did not understand what humility meant or what it meant to be in touch with one's feelings. My faith and my understanding of my faith have grown and matured tremendously. Now, I am not as afraid of my feelings, understanding them and trying to make sense of them; I feel more comfortable with who I am and possess less need for other's approval.

My prior perception of feelings was that they were, for the most part, something to keep hidden—at least those feelings perceived as tender or "feminine." In my family, certain emotions/feelings needed to be suppressed—openly showing them was deemed a sign of weakness. It was acceptable to express anger but not to cry; to express elation but not to show pain or sadness. Now, expressing feelings, even discussing them in large groups, is not only not intimidating but enlightening. I find discussing with others opens insight into self and greater understanding.

Ministry must begin with a relationship with God, through the Holy Spirit acting in and through us. A relationship with God entails an active prayer life, an ongoing dialog with God, especially listening. It must precede any self-analysis around ministry or discipleship for God.

I had thought my prayer life was in good shape. In the Aspirancy Year, though, it became much richer and more meaningful. It was as if I was involved in "chit chat" with God before, and now I am able to enter into much deeper exchanges—reaching a higher plateau, a much higher level of intimacy, and bonding spiritually.

I discovered that prayer is not just a conversation with God; instead, prayer is communication with God—a big difference. Communication is central to any relationship and involves words, actions, body language, and an understanding of the other person. It is a closed loop—the better the communication, the better the relationship; the better the relationship, the better the communication. Each feeds on the other, forming an upward spiral, an upward tightening spiral. The spiral tightens as the relationship becomes more intimate while the communication becomes deeper at each level. Your trust in God becomes greater, as does His expectations of us.

This process needs to be primed or seeded. Very few of us are born communicators. It is a skill that has to be learned and developed. Some have greater capacities for conversation, but they, too, must develop this gift to become effective communicators. Since Christian prayer is communication, albeit communication with God, it too must be learned, developed, and practiced, becoming an essential part of daily ritual.

For the Holy Spirit to work through us, we need to be open to His message. This can only occur through an active prayer life, prayerfully reading scripture and reflecting on its message—recognizing that consistency of message requires full communion with the Lord, communion with the Body of Christ as well as with Christ. Fiorenza observed that, "I have noted that communion in the New Testament refers primarily to the vertical relationship between believer (as member in a community) and redeeming God. Modern theological usage more commonly employs the term to describe the horizontal or ecclesiological implications of the church's charismatic structure, shared responsibility, and collective accountability"(36). In practice, this communion about which Fiorenza writes has not been my experience as a post-Vatican II convert to the Catholic Faith. Both relationships—horizontal and vertical—have been emphasized, which is as it should be. The deeper the sharing and the more intimate and trusting the relationship, the clearer God's message becomes. Love of God results in actions/service, and action/service leads to a greater love of God.

Paragraph 2559 of the *Catechism of the Catholic Church* defines prayer as "the raising of one's mind and heart to God or the requesting of good things from God." The *Catechism* further refines this definition by providing the types of prayer–Blessings and Adoration, Prayers of Petition, Prayers of Intercession, Prayers of Thanksgiving, and Prayers of Praise—and their definitions. It then defines three expressions of prayer—vocal prayer, meditation, or contemplative prayer. Deeds and actions should be added as an expression of prayer. In human communication, only a small amount of communication is conveyed via words. More comes from the way it is said (voice inflections) and body language—in other words, you cannot not communicate.

The same concept is true of communication with God. Vocal, meditative, and contemplative prayer, all involve cerebral activity (or should) and in one form or another are conversations with God—words or thoughts. As in human communications, these modes comprise only a small portion of our total prayer. Much more comes from our body language, i.e., the way we live and conduct our lives, our actions, our ministries as we live our lives, navigating the choices of our faith journey. A major difference, though, is that God knows our hearts, and He knows our thoughts. So, while it may be possible to mislead or deceive a person, it is not possible with God.

Thus, while words and thoughts are an important part of prayer, but the greater part is our actions and deeds, how we live out our Christian principles and values, and how we communicate with God in all aspects of our lives. Our entire being is a prayer in that it communicates the essences of who we are: the real you before the real God.

But it is through the prayer of thoughts and words—vocal, meditative, and/or contemplative—that the strength and knowledge of faith comes to live a Christian example. The *Catechism* provides a formula for enriching the process; St. Ignatius, whose spirituality was the focus of the first year of the formation process, provides the fertile soil and nourishment to grow it into a mature faith, a complete prayer of mind and body.

Our personal development, to come in closer communion with God, requires that we continually practice traditional prayer, the Sacraments, and attend Mass. Reading scripture, introspection, expressions of thanksgiving and affection, and adoration and praise of God are all essential elements to grow in Faith and to bring us to the point of living a full Christian existence. A full Christian existence, however, entails not only the internal components of communication with God and public exhortations at Mass and Church-sponsored events, but it is also putting into practice the guiding principles of the faith in all aspects of our lives—practicing the stewardship of giving of our time, talents, and treasure to the support of the Church, and evangelizing others with the example of our lives and, also, with ministries in God's service. Once you understand your mission as a Christian, evangelizing and utilizing our charisms in various ministries become more natural and less forced and, therefore, easier. That is why it is essential to develop the traditional concepts of Prayer.

St. Augustine described prayer as, "Man is a beggar before God." Unfortunately, I was unable to find the context in which this quotation appeared. I personally do not, however, believe this sentiment. God did not create us to be beggars through prayer; prayer is for communication with God. Not just asking but to praise and gain understanding—to come into communion with Him. The more this union develops, the more we become attuned to God, and the more we trust in Him, allowing His will to work through us.

As deacons, we must fully embrace this concept of relationships and continually strive to grow in our relationship with God through self-knowledge by understanding and knowing our strengths and weaknesses—our charisms and gifts. We must actively seek and respond to God's call to ministry by reaching out to our fellow parishioners to help them recognize, develop, and act on their charisms and gifts in service to God. Through God's grace, all are called through baptism to priesthood and a life of service—"[. . .] spirituality for ministry is a bridge between the baptized and their services" (O'Meara 225). Even Jesus began His public ministry with His baptism in the Jordan by John the Baptist. Ministry is accepting God's call through baptism in water and the Holy Spirit.

Obviously, the Holy Spirit is active in the Body of Christ, prompting and promoting growth through change. In the early Church, all were called to ministry in all areas of the Church: "The theology of the Body of Christ indicates that ministry for the baptized should be ordinary: history indicates that the ministries of women have existed; the present age has affected a model that goes beyond the sole performance of whatever was being done by clergy or by religious and priest" (O'Meara 32). Vatican II has nudged the Church in that direction once more, but it will take time to regain comparable recognition of ministry for all in the Body of Christ as existed in the early Church.

As persons of free will, we make choices, and those choices result in experiences that influence who we are and why we do the things we do; they provide the foundation or principles on which we base our life, i.e., one's philosophy derives from his or her experiences. This philosophy, in turn, influences future decisions or choices.

For me, faith in God focused my life and sharpened my awareness, clarifying what should be valued versus what is superficial; it brought an inner peace and comfort with self. The inner yearning now channeled energies differently. They were no longer nagging feelings of doubt and self-worth that needed external recognition but positive energies directed at learning more about God and His Church, recognition that self-respect—values and the way a person lives his life—was really what mattered. This epiphany gave me a sense of purpose, shifting my aspirations from trying to live a life according to the expectations of others to living a life more closely aligned with Christ and His mission.

Essentially, I have come to the conclusion that people are wired differently—they have differing charisms, desires, and talents. Some have innate abilities in math, others in reasoning or logic, some with music, some with words, and some (probably most) are multi-talented. And, apparently, some of us have been wired to serve God directly through ministry. Unfortunately, many of us do not come to this awareness until later in life, spending our early years pulled toward careers motivated by money and prestige. We either do not know what we love, or, perhaps, we do not perceive that having a passion for something is necessary so long as it meets our other criteria. We make choices that may initially or permanently lead us in a direction away from what is life-giving. Perhaps, though, in God's wisdom, this path is by design. Maybe we need time to mature, experience life, and/or learn skills that can be used in His service. Either way, we can be certain that God does not give up and that the Holy Spirit is untiring in His efforts to bring us to Christ. We just have to be receptive.

Filled with the knowledge that God would lead me in a purposeful life, if I let Him, the hollowness was gone, replaced by an obsession to understand. Many people in the Church seem to be of this same mind set. They desire to understand and to learn more about their faith, but they do not know how to go about doing it or do not have the self discipline on their own. One of the ministries I feel called to is providing opportunities for adult Catholics to grow in their faith, and by doing so, they will willingly carry the Gospel to others.

Equipping lay people with the knowledge of their faith makes them better disciples for Christ. Catholics who live their faith and who are able to articulate its message clearly and with ease can not only affirm their faith by example, but they are able to communicate Christ's message of salvation with enthusiasm when called upon to do so. Catholics, as citizens of secular communities, influence public policy through the Christian principles and values they bring into the voting booth: "In this way they make Christ known to others [. . .] (*Lumen Gentium* #31). Vatican II made explicit the interconnection between the sacraments and the lay apostolate: "The apostolate of the laity is a sharing in the salvific life of the Church. Through baptism and confirmation all are appointed to this apostolate by the Lord Himself" (McGonigle and Tkacik 26). Thus, the reach and the effectiveness of the message are not only greatly enhanced, but the approach is consistent with what God has called each of us to do as baptized Catholics.

An informed laity creates a "ripple" effect, moving outward from the Church's center—Christ, touching more and more lives as the circle broadens. It knows no boundaries, as it reaches into all cultures, faith communities, and secular societies. Consequently, sensitivity to this diverseness must be maintained without diluting Christ's message of salvation with local customs and practices. What people associate with us as Catholics, they associate with the Catholic faith and the Church as a whole: "To be a sacrament of Christ to the world, the Church must serve as a symbol within the world that points to and makes Christ present. Since the Church's presence in the midst of the world is perpetuated by the lay faithful, they must serve as symbols which make Christ present to the world" (McGonigle and Tkacik 21). As ambassadors for Christ, we need to be constantly cognizant of the Church as a sacrament. The image we portray is the image people associate with the Church and with God.

According to Thomas McGonigle and Michael Tkacik in *Pneumatic Correctives*, "Vatican II set as the primary aim of liturgical reform the active participation of all of the faithful. To be true to this objective, a greater appreciation for the unity of all ministries within the church being rooted in and stemming from baptism is needed. The tendency toward ontological polarization between clergy and laity as a result of the character of Orders must give way to a vision of ministry united in the common and shared dignity of baptism and differentiated not by ontological status, powers, privileges and prerogatives, but by the service that the ministerial charism renders in the life experience of the worshiping community. Such a vision of ministry is in harmony with Christ's own example of ministry as service and Paul's understanding of ministry as slavery unto Jesus" (47). Thus, it was not so much a "new" concept as a return to practices more closely aligned with the early Church: "The Pneumatic corrective proffered by the Liturgical Movement and the Second Vatican Council called for the Church to recover these truths about liturgical worship" (McGonigle and Tkacik 33). Over the centuries, the chasm between the laity and the priest grew until, eventually, the laity became merely passive observers of the priest as he worshipped God. The liturgical movement, beginning in the mid-nineteenth century, identified this polarization and initiated the process of changing the liturgy to incorporate the entire "Body of Christ" in the Liturgy. A recognition that the "common and shared dignity of baptism" necessitated a rethinking of current practices in light of the entire history and practices of the Church, not only those behaviors during the last thousand years or so.

It is through our baptism that "[...] we are formed in the likeness of Christ [...] all of us are made members of Christ's body [...] in the building up of Christ's body various members and functions have their part to play [...] Christ continually distributes in His body [...] gifts of ministries in which, by His own power, we serve each other unto salvation" (McGonigle and Tkacik 15). "The body of Christ" speaks to the Eucharist but also to the people who are the body of the Church of which Christ is the head. Thus, the Church consists of the laity as well as the priestly, all baptized people of faith, and all are charged by Christ to carry forward His salvific message.

Where do people today make contact with the risen, glorified Christ and, through him, with God and God's saving grace? They do so in and through the community of the Church, as it exists now as the Spirit-filled

Body of Christ. We, the faithful, are the Church, with a mission to present to the world, Jesus, the head of the Church who is lovingly active in the world through us. "The New Testament is more likely to speak of "mystery" where we would employ the general notion of sacrament. In Paul's writings "mystery" is dynamic saving work of God that is revealed in Christ and that has already touched the lives of those who believe (e.g., 1 Cor 2:7–10; Col 1:26–27)" (LaCugna 192). As individuals, Christ is reflected in our daily activities, deeds and words; as a community, Christ is reflected through the unified body of the Church in societal issues of social justice, morality, and in caring for the gifts of our world. We must always be guided and be defined by the principles of our faith.

The task of the Church is to be a sign of Christ that people understand and recognize, as well as a sign of intimate union with God and with all of humanity because of the Church's relationship to Jesus. Through the deeds, words, and actions of the Church community, non-Christians and non-Catholic Christians alike will form their opinions of Catholics and the Christian Faith. It is through us that Jesus reveals himself to the world. People should recognize the in-dwelling Spirit of Christ and the benefits of Christianity through our conduct. As Christians, we must remember that we are always ambassadors for Christ and His Church, and that "the Church as a basic sacrament is a real sign and symbol of God's love for humanity and the human love of God" (Fiorenza 329).

As Catholic Christians, we live in the secular world. Through the daily processes of living, we continually come in contact with marginal Christians as well as those who have had no exposure to Christ or His salvific message. These "touch points" are our opportunities to bring Christ to them through our words and deeds, i.e., we inspire and motivate Christ-like behavior by being Christ-like. Christ is contagious, not only among non-Catholics but Catholics as well; many people will be inspired to action if we model the love that Christ personifies: "[. . .] The Church—that is, the kingdom of Christ already present in mystery—grows visibly through the power of God in the world. [. . .] All men are called to this union with Christ, who is the light of the world, from whom we go forth, through whom we live, and towards whom our whole life is directed"(*Vatican Council II* 351).

By sheer numbers alone, and with the more intimate exposure to secular society, it is clear the laity must carry "[. . .] the vision of the Church as the sacrament of the Paschal Mystery characterized by a mission and ministry of service unto the world [. . .]" (McGonigle and Tkacik 57). And as ordained ministers of the Church, it is paramount that we, as deacons, recognize that "a minister without prudence is a danger to the church. Good judgment is not a luxury in ministry; it is an absolute necessity" (O'Meara 238). Also, as deacons with one foot in the secular world and one foot in the Church, "[. . .] there should be too a spirituality of the permanent deacon who today bridges liturgy and service, ordinary life and ministry" (O'Meara 236). We need a deep knowledge of our faith tempered by a vibrant spirituality to be effective ministers for Christ—"[. . .] a theology of Grace personalized" (O'Meara 232).

Being a "Sacramental Faith," the sacraments must attain a greater presence in the consciousness of all Catholics. It is through the sacraments that we grow spiritually as individuals and as a community. The sacraments, therefore, should be received in community when possible. This is especially the case with infant baptism. Just as adults are received in to the community at the Easter Vigil Mass, infants should be received in at Mass in front of the entire community. All Catholics need to be reminded of their commitment, covenant, and responsibilities as Catholics, specifically their responsibilities to the newly-baptized.

According to O'Meara, "ministry is: (1) doing something; (2) for the advent and presence of the kingdom of God; (3) in public; (4) on behalf of a Christian community; (5) as a gift received in faith, baptism, and ordination; and (6) as an activity with its own limits and identity existing within a diversity of ministerial actions" (141). Increasing the knowledge and awareness that other people have of their faith through adult formation and instruction certainly fits this definition—and could be rewarding. For me, though, I would also prefer some first-hand experience in helping those people who are on the fringes of our society and in most need of a spokesman. So, in addition to doing my small part to improve the adult formation within my parish and/or deanery, my greatest passion is the pro-life ministry. We, as Catholics, have steadily fought to repeal Roe vs. Wade and to restore a culture of life within our country.

Recently, I was challenged on this topic with the following question: "Why do you support bringing more unwanted children into the world, who, for the most part, will be neglected and uncared for and become a burden on society without looking for ways of making them into productive members of society?" A fair question. If you can demonstrate to an expectant woman that she can receive medical care throughout the pregnancy at no cost to her or to her family, and that the baby will not only not be a burden to her after he or she is born but go to a caring, loving family, many women might agree to carry the baby to term.

Shortly after this episode, I was listening to Dr. James Dobson on his show *Focus on the Family*. He had a guest, an Evangelical minister, who had started a ministry within his church for "Fee Free Adoptions." This program not only provides the cost of having a child, of identifying families for adopting it, and of bringing them together, but it also arranges for adoption of older children who are in the foster-care system or in orphanages. My hope is to initiate such a program in the Savannah area.

After discussing this with several people, including Deacon George Foster, director of the Permanent Diaconate Program for the Diocese of Savannah, who have been involved in setting up ministries of this type, I have learned that being affiliated with the Church could restrict fund raising from businesses, society at large, and government grants. It is my intent, though, to continue to explore the feasibility of making this idea a reality. I will spend the next couple of years learning more about the processes involved, developing a business plan, and acquiring the necessary support. The more I pray about this endeavor, the more I believe it is my calling. It is a ministry that truly touches my heart.

How can I be more Christ like? This question is the perennial one that has haunted Christians since the time of Christ. Martyrdom, monasticism, virginity, and poverty were perceived virtues of Christ that should be imitated, allowing one to live out the Gospels in a literal way. Martyrdom showed the devotion and obedience to the Father; monasticism, the single-mindedness of devoting your existence to God and His Word; virginity, maintaining purity of the flesh so as not to corrupt or weaken the spiritual devotion; poverty, to grow in humility and to ensure that the love of God was done with the whole person—body and soul. To me, the question of how to be more Christ-like is best addressed through practicing the servant-leadership role Christ lived during His time on earth. I aspire to take the meager talents I have and leverage them in a servant role to further Christ's mission.

So, why do I serve? For me, it is a way to feed my passion for God and to grow spiritually. Being around and interacting with like-minded people, contributing to causes that help the less fortunate, and/or being able to make a positive difference in someone's life, God permeates your whole being. One truly receives more than he or she gives—always.

Also, outreach to all peoples comes from recognition that it is the Holy Spirit who defines the global boundaries of the Church community and the body of Christ, not a specific Church affiliation. Local communities are microcosms of the larger Church and society. As such, we who are at the grass roots must be cognizant of this fact as we reach out with the Good News to others. Being cognizant does not preclude the fact that the majority of our service occurs, however, within the boundaries of our parishes and local communities. Christian service must begin here and emanate outward. Thus, the first order of business is fulfilling the spiritual and physical needs of our immediate communities. We should aspire to achieve harmony between Christ's example and ours and to understand and align His teachings with ours, i.e., living what we preach.

Essentially, Faith is Love. The deeper we sincerely love God, our fellow man, and self, the better we can understand how to be a servant leader. Our ministries should provide people hope, and we, as Christians, should be dream makers, not dream breakers. We should be life giving by faithfully following Jesus' example and His two great commandments—love God and love our fellow man. These should be the guiding principles in our life.

BIBLIOGRAPHY

Fiorenza, Francis S. "Systematic Theology: Tasks and Methods." *Systematic Theology: Roman Catholic Perspectives.* Vol. 1. Eds. Francis S.Fiorenza and John P. Galvin. Minneapolis, MN: Fortress Press, 1991.

———. "Marriage." "Systematic Theology: Tasks and Methods." *Systematic Theology: Roman Catholic Perspectives.* Vol. 2. Eds. Francis S.Fiorenza and John P. Galvin. Minneapolis, MN: Fortress Press, 1991.

LaCugna, Catherine Mowry. "The Trinitarian Mystery of God." *Systematic Theology: Roman Catholic Perspectives.* Vol. 1. Eds. Francis S.Fiorenza and John P. Galvin. Minneapolis, MN: Fortress Press, 1991.

McGonigle, Thomas C. and Michael Tkacik. *Pneumatic Correctives: What is the Spirit Saying to the Church of the 21st Century?* Lanham, MD: University Press of America, 2006.

O' Meara, Thomas F., O.P. *Theology of Ministry.* Mahwah, NJ: Paulist Press, 1999.

Rolheiser, Ronald, O.M.I. "The Struggle to Bless" *The Observer.* November 2007 http://observer.rockforddiocese.org/Columnists/FatherRonaldRolheiserOMIInExile.

Vatican Council II: Vol. 1 The Conciliar and Post Conciliar Documents. Ed. Austin Flannery. New York: Costello Publishing Company, 2004.

Deacon Don and Karen Coates
St. Joseph Catholic Church, Macon

Don Coates

"You are a very Spirit-filled minister who radiates the joy and enthusiasm of God. I am glad we are friends." In reflecting upon these words that my friend Fr. Michael Cooper wrote in a dedicatory, I wonder if God would say the same thing to me. Would God say to me that I reflect the joy and enthusiasm of His Son, Jesus? Would God call me a friend to all his children? As God sees me, my spirituality, and my ministry, would He see the face of all people? Am I serving God and his people through the love and spirit of His Son, Jesus?

Over the years, I have discovered how exhilarating in the love of the Lord service in church ministries can be. According to *Lumen Gentium*, "[. . .] the first and most necessary gift is charity, by which we love God above all things and our neighbor because of him." In the Initiation degree for the Knights of Columbus, there is a similar phrase that encapsulates the organization's purpose, that above and beyond everything else, charity is the foremost principle to which a Knight abides. As a member of the Order for thirty-seven years, and in communion with many Brother Knights, I have done my best to live by that principle. That communion with my Brother Knights motivates and excites me to seek out and serve those who are less fortunate, and to assist others in the myriad of programs the Knights support. For many years, I have felt called to serve on my Council's Church and Vocation committees. My service on these committees inspires me in other areas as well, especially the preparation of liturgies. It is in services to others where we can truly experience a felt sense of God. When I commit myself to service, I know that I am answering God's call to carry Him to other people.

There are two areas in particular where I have experienced most a call to serving and ministering. First, many years ago I attended a Cursillo weekend. It was exactly what I needed at that time in my life, because it was a spiritual assessment/regrouping for me that was long overdue. There is no doubt that the Holy Spirit led me to this experience. As a result, I have a much deeper sense of our Church community, and, in particular, I have experienced the beauty of the "Catholic" (universal) church through close associations with Catholics in the Philippines, France, and Nigeria. Second, my wife Karen and I have served our parishes (various Air Force assignments) in many roles over the years. Usually, I was on the Parish Council and Liturgical committees, and Karen served on women's groups. In spite of our service at the same churches, our roles and responsibilities never seemed to coincide so that we worked together. A comment made by Karen almost thirty years ago still resonates today in my conscience: "Do you realize that you have been to a church meeting five nights this week?" The unspoken subjects were family time and balance in life. What I call my "imbalance demon" still lurks, but in my life I feel that I have improved in my efforts to be the most effective minister to my family and the people I serve. I continue to ask myself, "What is the mission to which I am called?" Am I using my "gifts" in ministry to others?

A discerning question for me is, "If you are happy and fulfilled in your service to the Church now, why should I answer the call to be a deacon?" When I was a young boy, there was no doubt in a lot of other people's minds that I was destined to enter the priesthood. I remember once telling an adult that "the Church was my hobby." That's how much I enjoyed participating in the life of the Church. Now here is a humorous analogy. Throughout my senior high school year, our family participated in various church programs offered in the liturgical seasons. Following the Friday night programs, several of us teens would head to a local beer pub (we were eighteen years old and could drink beer). Guess what the topic of conversation usually was—the Church and everything about it. It was the mid-1960s, and we were in the midst of change. The Church was my training ground. Now, here I was, forty years later, going to the pub with a group of great guys and talking about this great God who has us all fired up to serve the Church and the people of God. Fast forward to that voice of conscience again. I was listening to a seminarian speak at Mass, and he said "that you have to respond to that voice that will not go away, and calls you to an action." He was referring to the priestly life for himself, but it was my wakeup call to respond to serve God and His Church as a deacon. As I reflect on the numerous parish committees and jobs over the years, I know this decision/action to serve the Church community in this role is where I am called. I feel at peace—worried and scared—but ready to serve. The Holy Spirit is at work in my life!

The first meeting of our diaconal formation was in September 2003. I vividly recall many of us, in sharing our life's experiences for the first time, talked about how "unworthy" we felt to be called to this ministry. Fr. Michael Cooper, who taught us our first year in the program, very strongly told us to stop thinking of ourselves as "unworthy," that "we are who we are." In addition, he told us "to savor our blessings." As I have reflected upon our first year together, I replay many of those moments that impacted me. How has my image of God changed? What have I learned about myself? What changes have taken place in my spirituality? As a class, my brother deacons and I had five years of blessings to savor. The best way to define the change we experienced is that we fell in love, with one another and, more so, with the Lord Jesus!

I wonder often, what is the one, all encompassing statement that defines me? It just so happened (Holy Spirit in action?) that the answer came to me while I was reading an article about the Latin Mass. According to the article, the Latin Mass distinguishes itself among world religions/faiths in that it is a definitional Catholic action. As Catholics, many of our actions define our beliefs, such as making sign of the cross and genuflecting. I keep thinking that being "Catholic" is how I want to be defined. To me, it means that the love of God, through His son Jesus and the work of the Holy Spirit, is reflected in and by me in my actions and associations with people. It would be a beautiful tribute to a person if someone who noticed the loving God-filled radiance in you, would ask you where that joy has its origin.

I always want to be a joyful person. That does not mean that I mask or ignore the pain that I have experienced or will encounter in life. Be happy! I want to die a happy man. I want the inscription on my tombstone to read, "He died a happy man—in Christ!" Over the years it has become a "battle cry" of my children. When we are in the midst of life's decisions, we always return to what is most important, and that is no matter what decision is made, it must be one that brings happiness. Life is too short to be unhappy. And that is how I like to go about my ministry. There is good in every situation, and there is God in every situation. "The glass is half-full!" When I work with friends, faculty, students, or anyone, I try to always think that what we are doing not only is positive and good, but it is also life-giving. A wonderful Mercy Sister always reminds me that "what you are doing at every moment is the most holy thing that God wants you to be doing."

Jesus Christ and his message are alive in us today. This philosophy is the Ignatian vision of "finding God in all things." God has a plan for each of us. As we discern events, activities, and decisions in our life to serve God and others, Ignatian spirituality tells us that God has already started the process. God has found us: "you are precious in my eyes." We need to find God, and there we will find and experience joy.

According to *Gaudium et Spes*, the nature of humanity is more clearly revealed and new roads to truth are opened in various forms of human culture, and this diversity profits the Church. I want to share two personal scenarios that reflect this vision. When I lived in the Philippines for several years, I was actively involved in parish life and outreach programs to the Filipino people. By far, the people whom I encountered were practicing Catholics, and they were mostly "the poor and the afflicted." Yet they had deep trust and faith in the Catholic Church, in addition to a passionate hope that things would always work out for the best. Furthermore, they were always at peace and lived joyful lives. The National Catholic Educational Association (NCEA) conventions I have attended in various cities have afforded me the opportunity to experience closely the cultural differences of thousands of Catholics from many different countries and states. It is a unique feeling and appreciation when one belongs to a truly universal church. This awareness has affected me, inspiring me to embrace more fully people of all cultures and to truly experience the face of God in others.

I have the opportunity to be involved in planning many different kinds of liturgical services for my parish and the school where I am employed as the campus minister. I am passionate about planning and serving liturgies, and I do genuinely feel that this love of service is a gift from God. I am inspired when I study the special seasonal liturgies of our church, help bring a team together, and educate and train other people for the purpose of worshiping and glorifying God. I am inspired when I see people, especially students, beam with the love of the Lord as they lead others in prayer. For many years, I have felt a strong call to help people take active roles in our liturgies. I know that I have felt the true presence of God within me as I have witnessed people lead and participate in inspirational ways. I am cautious, however, about a trap that Karen helped me to see. Once, when I was excitedly talking about a liturgy she said to me, "It sounds as if the liturgy was beautiful, but where was 'your' prayer and not just logistics in the program?"

Now, I am in the midst of practicing and serving at the Latin Mass offered in our parish, and, at the moment, there are only three of us who know the altar boy's responses and actions. This is an important occasion for me. As an educated adult who is immersed in the Church since Vatican II, I have grown to understand, appreciate and love more than ever what we experienced years ago in the Latin Mass. Consequently, I feel like I possess a greater understanding and appreciation of the faith and traditions of our Church, while we move forward in implementing Vatican II initiatives. We grow through our traditions. There is room for all of us at the table, and "all are welcome".

The diaconal formation program, and especially the first year of spiritual formation, changed my prayer life. My personal prayer life could have been described as repetitive and somewhat passionless. Today, I pray more often and in different ways. My prayers are much more, and in my daily actions I know I have more conversations with the Lord. I am so much more keenly aware that everything I do or have is a gift from God. I have learned to "take it to the Lord," and I am not ashamed to say that on many occasions I just "give it to the Lord." I cannot deal, nor do I want to, with many issues or situations over which I have no control. I think those moments have been and will continue to be "grace-filled" experiences for me. I have learned that I am not in control of anything and that God has the control. The freedom and peace that are the result of praying that God remove my burdens from me are true blessings.

In Fr. Michael Buckley's article "Because Beset With Weakness," he states that by weakness he does not mean the experience of sin, but "weakness is the experience of a peculiar liability to suffering [. . .] an inability to perform as we should want [. . .] to ward off [. . .] anguish" (Buckley 125-126). In reflecting upon these words there are areas that concern me, worry me some, and give me a little bit of anguish. Maybe, these feelings are the result of the awesome calling from God to serve Him and His Church. I can hear the words of my friend Fr. Michael Cooper, whose recommendation for my brother deacons and me during moments of uncertainty or weakness was, "Stay with this concern and take it to the Lord." Buckley tells us that we must be liable to suffering and weakness, because we must become what we touch—the body of Christ, the people of God. Am I God's hands, His feet, His heart, His unconditional loving embrace to my brothers and sisters? Am I there to listen and to act upon the cry of the poor and the marginalized? We experience the joys and sufferings of others. We struggle, we make mistakes, we are fearful, we fear death, and we question the meaning of life: "Weakness more profoundly relates us to God. We see his grace, his sustaining presence reveals itself, and his power can become manifest" (Buckley 127). Buckley, whose article is directed toward priests but contains valuable insight for all people who answer God's call, writes that "we have made a costly choice to become priests, and we should not disguise that choice. Neither should we disguise the love we are about [. . .]" (129).

With all my might, I want to be a deacon who ministers perfectly at all times, but I know that this desire is impossible and not practical. I am going to sin (less, I hope), and I am not always going to give a stirring homily to all (yet maybe a few). My spontaneous public prayer may not be the most moving and eloquently spoken, and I know I will not have the answers each time when asked about the Church's rules and positions. In spite of my concerns, I find strength in the knowledge that our loving

God is at work in us—his power and love can do more than we could ever hope or imagine in amazing and unexpected ways.

What is God's dream for me? What is his ordained "individual particular will" for me? I know that God loves me, and He waits patiently for me to return to His graces when I have sinned. I know in my heart that God truly accepts me no matter what I do. His love is infinite!

I have grown spiritually and have developed a deeper sense of personal character since I answered God's call to serve Him as a deacon. I think that I am doing a better job of seeing Christ in all people. When listening to students and participating in events with them, I feel so much more at peace because I am really listening to them as they share their concerns, their ideas, and their excitement. I have moved away from trying to recommend actions or solve issues by some textbook approach. Similarly, walking away from a difficult or challenging situation is no longer my style. I know it is not my calling or my role to solve every problem or right every wrong, but it is my responsibility to help God's people, however and wherever He leads me.

I am fortunate, and I am blessed. Why did God give me to my parents and not to parents who are the poorest of the poor? What has He ordained for me? God started His plan for me a long time ago. My brother deacons and I have taken some small steps together, yet I believe our full potential to serve Him and our Church is just developing. We journey through each day as the Paschal Mystery—we suffer for our offenses, we die to sin and self, and we rise to new hopes and new beginnings. The five-year formation program was the "bloodless Paschal Mystery." The program itself was the "life;" the ordination was the "death" to the old ways; and now we are called to serve God and each other—that's the "resurrection." Praise the Lord. Amen.

BIBLIOGRAPHY

Buckley, Michael J. "Because Beset With Weakness…" *To Be A Priest: Perspectives on Vocation and Ordination*. Eds. Robert E. Terwilliger and Urban T. Holmes. New York: Seabury Press, 1975.

Van Breemen, Peter G, S.J. *As Bread that is Broken*. Denville, NJ: Dimension Books, 1974.

Deacon Kerry and Verna Diver
St. Teresa of Avila Catholic Church, Grovetown

Kerry Diver

WHEN I BEGAN THE diaconate formation program, I understood that the ministry of deacon was centered on service: service to God and service to my fellow man. I cannot say that my basic understanding has changed, but I now have a much richer knowledge of what is meant by service. Who am I to serve? How do I serve? What are the sources that nourish my ministry of service? These questions, and many more, have been answered by the education I received during the formation program.

As I focus on service, several scriptures come to mind. In Matthew 22, we are introduced to the Great Commandment: "You shall love the Lord, your God, with all your heart, with all your soul, and with all your mind. This is the greatest and the first commandment. The second is like it: You shall love your neighbor as yourself. The whole law and the prophets depend on these two commandments." The Great Commandment emphasizes the inseparability of the love of God and the love of neighbor/community. This commandment serves as a moral imperative and the backbone of Catholic social teaching, which instructs us to reach beyond ourselves.

Jesus teaches his disciples that to serve the Kingdom of God, one must interpret differently the social and religious convictions of first-century Israel: "[. . .] the last will be first, and the first will be last (Matt 20:28)". "[. . .] the Son of Man did not come to be served but to serve [. . .]" (Matt 20:16). Jesus provides an excellent example of servant leadership in John's narrative of the Last Supper, during which He washes the feet of His disciples:

> If I, therefore, the master and teacher, have washed your feet, you ought to wash one another's feet. I have given you a model to follow, so that as I have done for you, you should also do. Amen, amen, I say to you, no slave is greater than his master nor any messenger greater than the one who sent him (John 13:14–16).

Christian ministry and service must be grounded in the person of Jesus the Christ, who He was and who He is. Ministers and anyone who answers God's call to service must remain humble as He was, always in service to the God who created us and called us to His ministry. In addition, we must pray always that we act in a manner consistent with God's will for us, or as Karl Rahner would note, God's individual and particular will.

Theology is the explanation by the human subject of the encounter with the divine. A theology of ministry should logically begin with baptism, the initiation of one to the community of faithful. In *Theology of Ministry*, Father Thomas O'Meara notes that baptism is the principal sacrament of the ministry. One of the major accomplishments of Vatican II was the recognition of the baptismal dignity of the laity. Based on this baptismal dignity, the laity became more greatly involved in the Church, both sacramentally and through mission. *Lumen Gentium* states, "[These faithful] are in their own way made sharers in the priestly, prophetical, and kingly functions of Christ; and they carry out for their own part the mission of the whole Christian people in the Church and in the world"

(*Lumen Gentium* #31). Through baptism we all become a royal priesthood. *Lumen Gentium* also speaks of the holiness of the people of God: "The baptized, by regeneration and the anointing of the Holy Spirit are consecrated as a spiritual house and a holy priesthood" (*Lumen Gentium* #10). O'Meara emphasizes that this is not a sacerdotal priesthood but priesthood in service to the gospel and the Kingdom of God. O'Meara posits that the contemporary expansion of ministry stems from this deeper understanding of baptism.

Vatican II also elevated the status of the laity within the Church by the understanding of Church as the people of God: "These faithful [laity] are by baptism made one body with Christ and are constituted among the People of God [. . .]" (*Lumen Gentium* #31). Acknowledgment of the faithful as the People of God begins to tear down the barriers an inequality between the clergy and laity created.

I have found it useful to view baptism as an initiation into the community of Christians and not simply the forgiveness of original sin. This interpretation takes on more importance when we view baptism as a process and not as an event. This viewpoint can also be applied to the other sacraments. We are nourished on our pilgrimage, our spiritual journey, by grace and a grace-filled community—grace being the living and loving presence of God in each of us, our community, and our Church.

My understanding of a theology of ministry is significantly enhanced by focusing on the Holy Spirit. Following the Ascension, Christ is present in the person of the Holy Spirit, the Spirit of Jesus and God (Holy Trinity). O'Meara states, "By baptism that spirit is present as a source of a new life where every Christian is a new creation, a full member of the people, a part of a living Temple" (O'Meara 201). The forces, both human and divine, that lead a Christian into ministry draw on the individual personality and the life of the Holy Spirit begun by baptism. This concept is important to me, that my call to ministry, although clearly the initiative of God, depends greatly on my individual make-up and personality. The Spirit enhances our God-given potentialities to bring us into fullness as a person; our model of the perfect human being Jesus.

The Holy Spirit is the source of the individual communities, as well as the whole Church, and the Church is under the rule of the Spirit. It is the Holy Spirit that gives to individuals numerous gifts according to the measure of their faith. These gifts are multiple and diverse but are intended to be for the benefit of all and the edification of the Church. Through diversity (of gifts of the Spirit), we achieve unity (one Church).

As a Church we are in constant need of reform and renewal. According to Yves Congar, the Holy Spirit is the vehicle through which "God communicates Himself to us, makes Himself active in us and thus enables us to perform actions of Christ [. . .] The Spirit plays a decisive part in building up the Church" (qtd. in McGonigle and Tkacik 2). As a missionary Church we must remain open to the demands of society and diverse cultures, and we must remain open and faithful to the lead of the Holy Spirit. Furthermore, we must remain willing to change, which Thomas McGonigle and Michael Tkacik describe as a "pneumatic corrective" in their book *Pneumatic Correctives: What is the Spirit Saying to the Church of the 21st Century?* A pneumatic corrective, according to McGonigle and Tkacik, occurs "when the Holy Spirit, through prophetic voices in the Church, calls for a reinterpretation of a text and/or teaching that more fully corresponds to the truth of the Apostolic faith" (McGonigle and Tkacik 3). As a minister of God, we must always be receptive to the promptings of the Holy Spirit.

Before I leave the topic of the Holy Spirit, I would like to speak more of the gifts of the Holy Spirit, or charisms. Paul teaches us that God gives all of us charisms in order to build up the Church. There is no hierarchy of charisms, because all of them are important. Hans Kung saw charisms as universal and primal but not miraculous: "[charisms signify] the call of God, addressed to an individual, to a particular Ministry of the community, which brings with it the ability to fulfill that Ministry" (qtd. in O'Meara 204). O'Meara notes that "Charism ultimately is grace; as such it is a dialogue, a conversation between the spirit and an individual Christian. Charism is not the creation or possession of the individual Christian, because charism is God's gift, the active presence of the kingdom of God permeating an individual, and charisms respect the sovereignty of God in the individuality of the person" (O'Meara 205). Charism is the source and foundation of every Ministry and such is diaconal, linked to service. Ministry is not a product of the Church but results from the action of the Spirit in the community.

A third concept that has influenced my theology of ministry has been that of Church as Community. Genesis 1:26 instructs that man is created in the image and likeness of God. Most see this teaching as relating to people as rational and volitional beings, but people are also social and relational beings. By the nature of our creation, we were not meant to be alone but in relationships, assembled into groups and communities. Scripture is rich with this concept of community as seen in the Old Testament understanding of covenant.

Jesus' Great Commandment, a condensation and fulfillment of the Decalogue, deals with how one should live in community. This concept of community that was so important in the early Church was lost following the fourth century. Vatican II was responsible for the rediscovery of this concept. We are a community of believers and, by our baptismal grace, the People of God. The Church is the People of God. Vatican II, as alluded to before, also rediscovered a communal aspect of the sacraments. The early Church believed that Jesus remained present to the community through His Spirit. These communities were empowered by the Spirit and dedicated to perpetuating the ministry of Christ. The Church is the community which responds in faith to Christ via their lifestyle (Faith and Works). The local church community is to be an environment which enables a new way of living:

CHURCH = COMMUNITY = FAITH = LIFESTYLE

Love characterizes this new mode of being community. Ordinary activities remain the same, but they are enacted with a new and different spirit.

Vatican II focused on local churches. The Council called for the local churches to be deeply rooted in their own cultures, in dialogue with other societies, and ecumenically responsive. Above all, the Council viewed the parish as a community of love rooted in the love of the Trinity that seeks the will of God, follows the path of Christ, and obeys the prompting of the Spirit. Rahner noted that it is the local church, the local community of believers, where Church is actualized.

Vatican II and its many documents have markedly influenced my theology of ministry. I fear the antiquarianism referred to by O'Meara is in progress with the pendulum swinging away from the post-conciliar reforms. Many recent actions of the Vatican give testimony to this truth. With Vatican II, there was a major change in the theology of the Church from the Classical Essentialist to the Historical Existentialist. This shift "made it easier for the Council Fathers to articulate the faith in a manner capable of being in relationship with the contemporary world" (McGonigle and Tkacik 11). The Council firmly places the Church within the lived experiences, history, culture, and existential conditions of our society, and the Church acknowledged that She is "subject to the historical demands and conditions of the times" and [. . .] must adapt and modify herself [. . .] if [the Church] is to be effective, meaningful and viable (*Lumen Gentium* #48 and *Gaudium et Spes* #s 39, 40, 57).

The Council noted that the Church and culture are mutually interdependent, and, therefore, theology must respect the cultural and historical context in which it finds itself (*Ad Gentes Divinitus* #22). The diversity of differing cultures contributes to and augments the Church's understanding of the Gospel and enhances her efforts in sharing it with others. The Council recognized that humanity comes to a true and full humanity only through culture (*Gaudium et Spes* #53). From the perspective of the Historical Existentialist, worldview revelation remains true; however, the way it is understood and expressed is conditioned by history and culture. This attitude is vital for the spread of the Gospel to new and culturally different people throughout our world. Just as the early Church adapted its ministry to the gentiles, we must be sensitive to new cultures that are hungry for the Word. Vatican II also affirmed the concept of Universal Salvation:

> While helping the world and receiving many benefits from it, the Church has a single intention: that God's kingdom may come, and that the salvation of the whole human race may come to pass. For every benefit which the People of God during its earthly pilgrimage can offer to the human family stems from the fact that the Church is "the universal sacrament of salvation (*Gaudium et Spes* #45).

Adherence to the doctrine that salvation can occur only through the Roman Catholic Church seems inconsistent with a loving and merciful God. Karl Rahner, as a Christian, accepts the presupposition that God has acted in the person of Jesus to save all mankind. Whenever one experiences God's saving action/truth/grace, therefore, one is experiencing Jesus.

Non-Christians, to the extent that they can, also experience God's saving action/truth/grace implicitly. According to Michael Tkacik, who was one of my professors in the formation program, salvation, therefore, is "inclusive of non-explicit Christian expressions of God's saving action/truth/grace" (Tkacik, In-class Notes). Furthermore, Jesus is "He who is God's saving action/truth/grace, and Jesus is therefore the constitutive element of these salvific expressions of God's saving action/truth/grace." By responding to God's saving action/truth/grace, one is in essence responding to Jesus even if they "are not explicitly aware of the fact" (Tkacik).

While recognizing the potential "of salvation outside of an explicit Christian faith, Rahner calls upon the Church to continue to evangelize so as to facilitate a process of spiritual maturation [and] to facilitate the time when what is experienced implicitly [...] will come to be experienced explicitly" (Tkacik, In-class Notes). Rahner's stance was not accepted by all Christians, some of whom accused him of religious relativism or a false theology. Rahner's detractors seem to misunderstand or simply miss, however, the centrality and universality of Christ in his theology. They also seem to forget Rahner's emphasis on evangelization (missionary activity) to develop an implicit understanding of Christ into an explicit awareness.

I believe this is what O'Meara is driving at in his discussion of minister as universal servant. He states that the minister needs to discern grace outside of the Church. The kingdom of God flows through the entire human race and all are called to be saved. The blood of the cross has objectively redeemed not only the baptized but the entire race. Grace is present in some modality or another as offered, received, or rejected within everyone. Christian ministry exists to make this presence explicit and to serve the kingdom of God.

My theology has also been shaped by Deacon George Foster's [Deacon George is the Diocese of Savannah's Director of the Permanent Diaconate] view of the diaconate as a ministry of healing. My experience of practicing medicine has helped me to recognize the prevalence of woundedness in our society. All Christians are called to serve and help these individuals, and we should never judge the people to whom we minister. Although it may be a cliché, the thought comes to me, "What would Jesus do?" Better yet, "What would Jesus want me to do?" I thank Deacon George for sharing stories from his ministry that have enabled me to answer these questions.

I would now like to discuss my spirituality of ministry, calling special attention to the spiritual experiences that have influenced my ministry. Spirituality, according to Father Michael Cooper in a class during the formation program, is discovering God's dream for us and living it to the fullest. Maas and O'Donnell note that, "an authentic Christian spirituality is one that binds us to Christ and leads us through the Holy Spirit to God the Father" (Maas and O'Donnell 17). Father Michael adds that, "spirituality is the inner and outer experience of being closer to God through the Holy Spirit." We are not alone on our journey but accompanied along the way by our Triune God.

O'Meara makes several useful points in understanding spirituality as it applies to ministry. A spirituality is a tradition and a school, and a group of beliefs about God and self. The spirituality I form will be mine, a personal spirituality specific for my ministry. A spirituality is a way of life and a way of seeing life. Our spirituality can not dwell in the "inner" but must bring forth action. A spirituality is, therefore, a theology of grace personalized. The spirituality of ministry will itself be diverse depending upon the social context of ministry. No one size fits all. O'Meara provides a very helpful insight, "[. . .] it is a sign of spiritual maturity to have had some contact with a great tradition of spirituality, and to draw from it and compose variations that enrich one's own spiritual life" (O'Meara 233). I must search and discover, with the help of the Spirit, a spirituality which works best for me and my ministry.

Clearly, the Aspirancy Year of the formation program, and specifically Ignatian Spirituality, had the greatest impact on my spirituality and ministry. The insights gained that first year have been immeasurable to me and my ministry, and I believe that many of the lasting memories of that first year of the program occurred during our first weekend, when my brother deacons and I shared our individual stories. I learned that God loves me just as I am—a sinner. God is not waiting for a perfected version of who I am, because He loves me with an unconditional love. He knew me before I was conceived, knitted me in my mother's womb, and I am precious in His eyes. Our call to ministry was totally the initiative of God, who called each one of us to service in His name. I feel confident that what I learned in the formation program, and especially during the Aspirancy Year, will continue to nourish me as I continue on my spiritual journey, which is a journey for life.

The Book of Genesis teaches God created us male and female and saw that we were very good: "God looked at everything he had made, and he found it very good" (Gen 1:31). Psalm 139 instructs, "You formed my inmost being; you knit me in my mother's womb. I praise you, so wonderfully you made me; wonderful are your works! My very self you knew" (Ps 139:13-14). I indeed felt and continue to feel special when I recall these scriptures. This sense of being special through God's love calls forth a deep sense of debt and gratitude. All of this results in a love of God which becomes the sole motivating factor in my life and ministry.

Yet, it is the numerous insights gained from our study of the Spiritual Exercises (SPEX) of St. Ignatius that have most significantly altered my life in both thought and action. The Principle and Foundation have taught me that we are personally loved by God, and through His love we are given gifts, talents, and blessings. These blessings are all true gifts, not earned or deserved. God's love and gifts are unconditional. There is nothing we can do to cause God to withdraw His love, and we are created to love and serve God so that we can attain the eternal salvation Jesus made possible. It is our choice, however, and it is a choice based on free will.

Week One of the Spiritual Exercises shows us that we are loved by God, even as sinners. It is sin that interferes with our ability to live "in union with God's faithful love." The light of the Principle and Foundation ("personally loved by the Creator who gifts") must give way to the darkness of Week One ("personally loved as a sinner by the Redeemer"). The SPEX introduced me to the concepts of consolation and desolation, the hills and valleys of our spiritual journey. I learned that desolation is the result of the confrontation of my sinfulness with the love of God and our salvation. Through perseverance in prayer and spiritual direction, we can overcome spiritual dryness.

In Week Two, I joined Christ on mission. The Gospel readings were experienced as "now events," the "Eternal now." I learned to approach the Gospels through Ignatian contemplation, and, consequently, I discovered God in unanticipated and surprising ways.

In Weeks Three and Four, I continued on mission with Christ through the Paschal Mystery and Resurrection. I followed Christ from "death to life." Christ's death and Resurrection empower me to deal with my personal struggles that occur in everyday life. By joining a laboring God on mission, these potentially death-dealing events are transformed into life.

I am impressed with the apostolic nature of Ignatian Spirituality, specifically the concept of God on mission. It is on mission where we meet God and God meets us: "Outer" → "Inner" →"Outer." Ignatian spirituality teaches us to take what we encounter in our everyday lives to the Lord in prayer. Although Ignatian spirituality is contemplative, it does not stop there. Action is favored over words. What we gain from our prayer life, "the inner," is applied or used for the benefit of our community, "the Outer." We move from the "Inner" to the "Outer" through prayer and discernment, where we meet God in action.

SPEX 230 teaches us that love should be manifested in action and deeds more than words. There is a dynamic equilibrium between love and service (action), which is the meaning of the inner → outer movement of Ignatian spirituality. This movement is best illustrated by the realization that Jesus lived a life that consisted of prayer (inner) and action/mission (outer).

The 'Contemplation to Attain Love' asks us to consider how God is actively laboring on our behalf. Spiritual Exercise 236, "He is working in the heavens, elements, plants, fruits, cattle, and all the rest—giving them their existence, conserving them [. . .]." In other words, we find God laboring in all things. God is always there ahead of us, and it is God who finds us.

Ignatian spirituality comes to fruition in the Suscipe, the prayer where we recognize that all is a gift from the unconditional love of the Father. We are so grateful to God that we realize that all we truly need is His Love: For us to love God and for God to love us. We freely give all to Him, asking that He use us according to His will. The intensity of this love is so overwhelming that it overflows into the love of our neighbor which we express through service to God and our community.

As my brother deacons and I studied Ignatian spirituality, we received many tools to help us on our spiritual journey. One of the most important was spiritual direction, which allows us to uncover the movements of God in our lives. A spiritual director does not give advice or solve problems, but rather he or she explores our feelings and emotions to discern the movement of the Holy Spirit in our lives. Spiritual direction allows a person to grow in intimacy with the Lord. As problems are encountered in spiritual direction, we are directed to take them to the Lord. SPEX 15 instructs us to let the creature deal with the Creator. Spiritual direction helps us to find the path to God, or more accurately, it clears the way for God to find us.

Week One of the SPEX asks the person to confront his or her disorderly attachments or affections, and instructs the person to become indifferent. These disordered affections are like chains that weigh us down and distance us from a personal relationship with our loving God. The concept of indifference to me is a state of balance where we try to keep all things in a proper perspective and priority. We avoid excesses in all things. Father

Michael Cooper's article titled "A Spirituality of Balance" examines the life of Sister Irene Dugan, who exemplified spiritual balance. As a person who lived life well grounded in her relationship with God, she was as comfortable wearing expensive French perfume as she was buying the cheapest brand of perfume from a neighborhood store.

The discernment of spirits has served me well over the past several years. What is life giving versus death dealing? Discernment takes place when a person searches within himself or herself to discover what brings lasting peace and joy. In addition, discernment enables us to recognize the spiritual forces within us so that we can weigh them as we seek to choose Good over Evil.

The concept of a "laboring God" invigorates me. We join God who is actively engaged, not distant or dispassionate, in our lives. The term 'disponability' describes our willingness to be available to the will of God. Are we willing to accept God's dream for us? This concept is expressed in the Suscipe, "[. . .] All of it is yours. Dispose of it according to your will."

"Deus Semper Major" demonstrates a God that is always more, always greater, and Lamentations 3:22-23 reinforces this concept for me: "The favors of the Lord are not exhausted; his mercies are not spent; They are renewed each morning, so great is his faithfulness." God wants us to know that there is always more for us. God is always "stretching" us, inviting us to be more. I now see God as my personal companion, closely at my side as I progress on my spiritual journey. I realize that God does not leave my side, although I frequently distance myself from Him. There are times when God, however, releases our hand, giving us "space to grow." I view periods of desolation as God giving us "room," and these times of aridity are God's invitation to a more intimate relationship. Esther Harding writes about "creative depression" in her excellent article, "*Value and Meaning of Depression*," and I believe we can strengthen our relationship with God when we experience this type of depression.

We are all unique in the eyes of God, so created through His love. O'Meara speaks of the human and divine intersection. It is this interaction which creates for us a personalized spirituality and ministry. Rahner notes that God communicates in a way that we may know his individual Will personally. God has an individual particular will, or dream, for each of us.

Rahner understood the action of the Holy Spirit in the mystical experiences and suggested that these mystical experiences were in the realm of possibility for all Christians. It is through the mysticism of daily life that we understand the Grace of God and its impact on our day to day existence.

Scripture is also of vital importance to my spirituality of ministry. I have already cited several passages from the Bible. The knowledge that God is always with me profoundly altered my day-to-day existence as I began to understand the personal closeness of God, my Father. I am empowered by the recognition that He never abandons us, though we sometimes distance ourselves from him. I am comforted by the words of St. Paul, in Romans 8:38–39: "For I am convinced that neither death, nor life, nor angels, nor principalities, nor present things, nor future things, nor powers, nor height, nor depth, nor any other creature will separate us from the love of God in Christ Jesus our Lord."

My approach to reading scripture has changed. Whereas I once viewed reading scripture as an academic quest, I consider it now an expression of my desire to understand what God is trying to say to me at this moment in time. As a "now event," I will meditate on a single passage and pray for the light of God's wisdom. I have grown to enjoy thoroughly the sharing of God's word with others as a faith-sharing experience and not as an academic exercise.

Prayer, as any exercise or activity that brings us into a closer relationship with God, is the life source of spirituality and ministry. My life in prayer has grown and matured since I answered God's call to serve Him as a deacon. We have been exposed to different types of prayer: vocal (Lord's Prayer, Liturgy of the Hours) and mental (*lectio divina*, meditative, and contemplative.) My most memorable events in prayer have come when I am silent in God's presence and listen attentively for Him to speak. Unfortunately, these are rare moments. As in life, we often become too busy too listen, even in our prayer life.

God seeks an intimate relationship with us through our prayer life. The article, "Praying Our Desires" by Father James Keegan, S.J., is inspirational. I learned that God wants a personal relationship with me, and He wants me to be passionate. Father Keegan's article taught me the courage to be the real me before the real God. I am able to approach God as an adult with real issues, issues that really mattered. When we approach God as an adult, He treats us accordingly. We are asked to pray with fervor and persistence. In the words of St. Irenaeus, "The glory of God is the human person fully alive."

St. Ignatius incorporated three forms of mental prayer into his prayer life: meditative, contemplative and the Examen of Conscience. George Aschenbrenner, in his article "The Consciousness Examen," notes that the examen prayer is an intensive exercise of discernment in one's life. The examen prayer must be interpreted in relationship to the discernment of spirits. This discernment primarily deals with the way in which the Lord meets us in the deepest recesses of our soul. Our actions, whether good or evil, are not the primary concern of the examen; rather, it is those movements deep in our consciousness that subsequently lead to the physical actions that are most important in discernment.

The effectiveness of the examen is linked to the quality of contemplative prayer in one's life. The spirit of Jesus within us fosters recognition that these inner movements lead us closer to God. This knowledge is a gift of God's grace, and we must learn to listen quietly if we truly are to hear the Lord speak to us. In the examen, we "pray to recognize God in even more subtle ways and to respond to his call with more faith, humility and courage" (Aschenbrenner 183). It has been this aspect of the examen that has been most helpful to me. I pray that God will allow me to see His face in all the people I meet and to feel his presence in all that I do. I ask that I will respond in a manner consistent with His Holy will and dream for me.

In addition to Ignatian Spirituality, I am also very impressed with the contemplative and meditative prayers of Teresa of Avila and Julian of Norwich. Other than the prayers of St Ignatius, however, it was the prayer life of Brother Lawrence of the Resurrection that most significantly altered my prayer life. His method of repetitive prayer, which constantly kept him in the presence of the Lord, is a method I have attempted to emulate.

I discussed earlier in my essay the numerous ways in which Vatican II shaped my theology of ministry. I believe Vatican II has also influenced greatly my spirituality. Vatican II celebrated the dignity of the human person based on his or her creation in the image and likeness of God. This concept was a theme of many of the documents of the Council. The inviolable dignity of conscience stems from the dignity of the human being. The conscience is the sanctuary and core where we are alone with God. The recognition of the Church as the People of God helped to rediscover the communal nature of our Church in sacrament and mission. Vatican II's emphasis on the local church as the place where "Church" is actualized enhanced my spirituality.

How do I see the different topics I have discussed unfolding in my specific ministry? How do I see myself as minister in my parish? O'Meara notes that we all are called to ministry. As we progress on our spiritual journey, we must recognize that God's call to serve Him is a key component of our spiritual being. When I began the diaconate formation program, I knew that a call to the permanent diaconate was a lifelong call to service. I now possess a more comprehensive picture of what service is all about due to the classes I had and the experiences my brother deacons and I shared. Service is more than assisting at Mass, an occasional homily, and adult or child education. It is more than hospital and home visits and counseling those in need of emotional and spiritual support. Although it includes all of these very important ministries, it is more: Service is an outreach to the community both at the local and global levels.

We must adhere to the platform of "Consistent Ethics for Life" as presented by Kenneth Overberg in his book *Conscience in Conflict* (Overberg 142). Overberg notes the issues that impact Catholic social justice are all interrelated. We cannot pick and choose issues as if they were a cafeteria plan. We must adopt all of the issues that protect, heal, and nourish life from cradle to grave. Furthermore, we must adopt Pope John Paul II's concept of "Preferential Option for the Poor." More than simply providing for the material needs of the poor and hungry, we need to see the world through their eyes. We need to correct the policies and institutions that result in inequality and thwart social justice, and we must support those actions that promote the common good.

I, and anyone who answers God's call, have very concrete responsibilities at the local level. O'Meara noted education is very important: "Like life in contemporary society, life in the church increasingly involves education. A spirituality of Ministry includes the desire to learn about the gospel, about the history of the church's expression of its faith, and about contemporary theology" (O'Meara 249). Sister Caroline Cerveny, SSJ, who taught a class on cyber culture in the formation program, emphasized the importance of knowing the people to whom we minister. Their desires and needs may be different than what we feel is required or important. We need to make our efforts meaningful to those present by enlisting their suggestions for topics and providing education at times that suits the people whom we serve.

I feel that building spirituality in a parish is the key to the success of every other parish endeavor. In my parish, we hope to build a new church and, at the same time, have taken the steps to becoming a total stewardship parish. In addition, we have the long-range goal of opening an elementary school. These ambitious goals will require the total support of the parish: emotionally, spiritually and financially. If we can make our parishioners aware of their giftedness through God's unconditional love, it is my hope that we can foster the response of gratitude, which will promote service and true stewardship. Toward this goal, I have entertained the idea of conducting an Ignatian Retreat in Everyday Life in our parish. A parish that is alive spiritually is capable of moving beyond concepts of obligatory participation to joyful celebration in the love of God. O'Meara emphasizes, "As ministry expands, formation and spiritual life must become deeper, more intense. The challenge is to let there be a constant dialogue between the ministry and the Christian spiritual life" (O'Meara 258). With the expansion of ministries in our parish education and spiritual growth will be necessities.

Spirituality and ministry are inextricably linked. A successful ministry is contingent upon a constant dialogue between ministry and Christian spirituality. O'Meara notes that, "A theology of Ministry is basically a meditation on the kingdom, a theology of the Holy Spirit, the contemplative analysis of grace" (O'Meara 38). Ministry finds its origin in the Christian community from which it flows and to whom it serves. O'Meara concisely summarizes the multiple aspects of ministry in his definition: "Christian ministry is the public activity of a baptized follower of Jesus Christ flowing from the Spirit's charism and an individual personality on behalf of a Christian community to proclaim, serve, and realize the Kingdom of God" (O'Meara 150). Ministry is service to others. It must be motivated by the love of God and facilitated by the grace of the Holy Spirit.

BIBLIOGRAPHY

Aschenbrenner, George. "Consciousness Examen." *Review for Religious* 31 (1972): 14–21.

Chittister, Joan, O.S.B. *The Rule of Benedict: Insights for the Ages.* New York: The Crossroad Publishing Company, 1992.

Cooper, Michael, S.J. "A Spirituality of Balance." *Spirituality in Depth: Essays in Honor of Sister Irene Dugan, RC.* Ed. Avis Clendenen. New York: Chiron Publications, 2002.

Harding, M. Esther. "The Value and Meaning of Depression." *Bulletin for the Analytical Psychology Club of New York* (1970): 113–35.

Ignatius of Loyola: Spiritual Exercises and Selected Works. Eds. Parmananda Divarkar, Edward J. Malatesta, et. al. New York: Paulist Press, 1991.

Maas, Robin and Gabriel O'Donnell, O.P. *Spiritual Traditions for the Contemporary Church*. Nashville: Abingdon Press, 1990.

McGonigle, Thomas C. and Michael Tkacik. *Pneumatic Correctives: What is the Spirit Saying to the Church of the 21st Century?* Lanham, MD: University Press of America, 2006.

O' Meara, Thomas F., O.P. *Theology of Ministry*. Mahwah, NJ: Paulist Press, 1999.

Overberg, Kenneth, S.J. *Conscience in Conflict: How to Make Moral Choices*. Cincinnati, OH: St. Anthony Messenger Press, 1989.

The Catholic Study Bible. Eds. Donald Senior and John J. Collins. New York: Oxford University Press (U.S.A.), 1990.

Vatican Council II: Vol. 1 The Conciliar and Post Conciliar Documents. Ed. Austin Flannery. New York: Costello Publishing Company, 2004.

Deacon Tom and Thalia Eden
St. Joseph Catholic Church, Macon

Tom Eden

I CONSIDER THE "THEOLOGY" of my ministry to be the foundation, which serves to support any other structure that I put into my ministry. Like a building, if I do not have a solid theological foundation, what I would seek to enhance in my ministry would be on shaky ground. I can also think of it as the "channel" (or boundaries) that I should and can stay within. My theology is fundamental and not situational or relative. There is a lot of freedom and room for creativity, but it also reminds me that there is a right and wrong.

I have heard people say that they are really not "into religion," but, rather, they practice "spirituality." This philosophy may appear trendy and cool, but in fact it is both lazy and dangerous. Are we to believe as individuals who live in the United States in the twenty-first century that we do not need any of the experience (tradition), knowledge and revelation (Scripture) that has been given to prior generations? Rather, we can sense what we "want" and what "feels good," and then rationalize that it is OK because it is part of our "spirituality." People who use this brand of spirituality to guide their lives do not find a God of their understanding, as they claim, but rather create a God for their convenience.

The two main elements of my theology are natural law and Scripture. Sometimes, one is ahead of the other, but they complement one another. Since I am a very logical person who rarely sees any conflict with the combination of Scripture and natural law, with a dash of the "mystical" added, it works well for me. I have found that when I read Scripture, honestly reflect on my experiences and the particular situation, and then wait quietly for God's answer, it comes together. A simple example is honesty, as sometimes opposed to technical "truthfulness." It is based in God's Law and Scripture, consistent with natural law, and when faced with a decision, it is reinforced by God's whispering guidance.

An example of this "theological" (Theo = God + logical→Godlogical) base for me can be seen in my journey to the diaconate. I have spent most of my adult life as a business manager and family person. I earned promotions, made more money and moved around the country—all in the name of trying to get more "stuff" and find self-satisfaction and contentment. The more I ran after this societal idea of "making it," the farther away I seemed to be, as measured by my waning inner peace. I was doing the "manlogical- or societalogical-" accepted approach, but it was very unfulfilling. I was not greedy or unethical. I was attending church on a regular basis, but without Scripture and mystical elements of my spirituality, I really was not on solid ground for any growth. (I did try seeking escape by immersing myself in my job and in the comfort of alcohol, but somehow neither one worked for the long term.)

After I had a God mandated and guided "course correction" (you can probably tell I am a sales and marketing guy; I am able to make a really ugly situation sound almost innocuous), I began to see the "holes" in my primarily worldly-driven "theology." I began to ask myself: What was my "purpose" and what were my "values?" What will I leave behind that will make any difference? Thus, I began to ask God for His direction, rather than be driven by the "expectations" of others, or use someone else's yardstick to measure my progress and worth.

To answer that question, I turned to the beginning, namely what are my talents? In Matthew 25:14, Jesus tells us that we will be accountable for how we use the talents we are given. I have been given good intelligence, logic and the ability to listen to others and then figure out what I have that can be of service (These are also the same sales and marketing skills that I had practiced for many years.).

Another important aspect of my theology is the fully-human Jesus Christ. Many times, especially during Mass and church services, we are only reminded of Jesus' divinity. He was also fully human. He laughed and cried. By sharing in our humanity, God wants us to know how much He loves and cares for each one of us as human beings. Jesus had a sense of humor (e.g. "the plank in your eye versus the splinter in someone else's," and "the blind leading the blind" are early Mediterranean knee slappers!). I have a sense of humor, and when appropriate, it can be very useful to put people at ease and to reach them.

I asked God to guide me to do what He wanted me to do. I kept coming back to the message: "Be a part of the solution of the problem that most bothers you." What hit me between the eyes was the phoniness and hypocrisy in the world, and that people thought they had to be that way to survive, or alternatively they sought escape through substances. Can I help people understand the love and acceptance of God as He made them, and still be content and experience peace and serenity?

First, I had to have it "together," or at least be well on track, in order to be able to convince others. One of the key pillars of continued recovery is service to others; namely, the concept of "giving it away to keep it." You cannot give away what you do not have yourself. Attraction, having someone think, "I want what they have," beats the promotion and preaching of an idea every time. By this time in my life, I had been studying Scripture in a Bible Study class, as well as practicing the twelve steps in my life. Without going into a long dissertation about how the steps are founded in the Bible, I easily concluded that they enhance one another. At that point, I began to understand and appreciate my God-given gifts. In addition, I was learning more about Scripture and saw how my life experiences could help me discover my purpose.

What ministry in the service to God and others should I do to use my gifts to help others who were restless, irritable and discontent? How could I bridge the gap many people saw existed between religion and living a good, fulfilling and practical life? After much prayer and meditation (listening for the answer), I felt called to inquire about the diaconate program. When I spoke to a priest about the deacon program, I learned that a new class may be forming in the next year or two, and I was given the contact information for the diocesan diaconate director. (It is fortunate that I initiated the conversation with the priest about the program. I was not really actively involved in any parish ministries and doubt that I would have been approached by any of the Macon church pastors.) During my period of discernment, I learned to "Let go and let God." The Lord has changed my life and done for me what I could not do for myself, but for what purpose? Do the footwork and the right door will open when the time is right. This concept is a simple one, but one that is not always easy to follow.

After two-three years in the diaconate training program, I began to understand more about my talents and how they can be of benefit to others. During the same time, I started to do some volunteer work with the poor. (Imagine a lifelong free-market capitalist, ex-executive working with people who had no idea how to manage a checking account or form and operate on a budget. Whodda thunk it?) Then, I reached the conclusion that my preconceptions are of limited use when following God's will. It was not clear what course I was to take, but it was clear that I was not called on to play a "role." I needed to be myself regardless of God's plans for my ministry. Currently, I am working as the business manager for two recently merged ministries that serve the young, low income families in Middle Georgia. Somehow, God has matched my talents with a real need in the community. Furthermore, I have been placed in a ministry that has other people with talents and gifts (e.g. empathy, feeling, extraversion) that I have not fully developed. It works!

Even as I continue to study and learn, I must always remind myself that Scripture is meant to be a "Now Event," not holy history. As a deacon, with many of the same experiences, family problems and struggles as the people I serve, I must take the theology and knowledge I have accumulated and help people relate the Bible to their everyday lives. God is not a one hour a week (Sunday Mass) God, but, rather, He can help us in our everyday lives—the other 23 hours and 6 days of each week. It is the deacon who ends Mass with the instructions, "Go in peace to love and serve the Lord." (More plainly, "You have heard the Word and been strengthened by the Eucharist, now go put it into practice!") This ministry of helping the laity connect the Church with their lives is very important to me. It helps overcome the "schizophrenic" Catholic tendency where many believe that religion is appropriate for Church time, but may not work well in our business and personal lives. Our religion and our values cannot be compartmentalized but must be integrated into our everyday lives.

We were taught throughout formation that the deacon's ministry is about love and healing. As a minister, we are to serve (Acts 6:1–6) and to love the people to whom we minister (John 13:34). The ministry of the deacon is not about wearing vestments and acting holy. If that is all that the people see, it can make the clergy seem aloof and unapproachable. Deacons are the bridge between the Church and the people of God, and for this reason, people must see us for who we truly are. We have made mistakes, and we have some successes—we are real. We share our experiences, strength and hope so that others may be better because of it. Through God's guidance, we can match calamity with serenity.

My objective is to acquire a depth of knowledge of scripture, tradition and doctrine that will help me to serve the people rather than complicate my ministry. KISS (Keep It Simple Stupid; I will be a deacon, not a junior priest.) Theology is most useful when it is used as needed to help others, not to impress them. I believe that I should do what is required and not complicate a situation with theological overkill. Major surgery is not required to heal a small cut.

Through training, the grace of ordination and personal prayer, I must remember to be guided by the Holy Spirit. If I rush in to a situation, I am doing so on my own. I should not try to do what is popular or what will make other people like me, for "Conformism leads to unplanned compromise." If I take time and act patiently (which is tough for me), and let the Spirit lead, the actions I take are on track and in tune with God's will.

During the five years of the diaconate formation program, I learned how to blend my education, gifts and ongoing personal experience. I have grown in my self-awareness, and I have learned that from a spiritual perspective, I am a "first floor" guy. Of the three main ministries performed by the deacon (Liturgy, Word, and Charity), I focus on Charity. The Liturgy will give me strength and the Word will give me direction, but most of my work will be with the poor, people who fight dangerous addiction, and people who battle despair and see little hope in their lives. Sounds like it might be a "downer," but I find this ministry incredibly rewarding and energizing.

I have discovered that I can be an instrument to instill hope to the downtrodden when I help them discover their own unique gifts. Many people whom I have worked with suffer from a feeling of frustration and lack of self confidence. First, I act with unconditional acceptance, followed by a dose of God's love, and finish with a plan to help them move ahead. I treat them without any expectations that they should apologize for who they are or what they have done (arrests, children out of wedlock, etc.). Together, we look at today, its situation and opportunities, and move forward. Most of what I do now is modeled after the Parable of the Good Samaritan (Luke 10:30–37). I aspire to help someone out of a tough situation (eviction, utility cut-off, etc.), then I place them into a situation that offers healing, confidence and hope (education, job training, and recovery), and, finally, I allow them to move on without me (empowerment). The real success can be measured by how many people no longer need my help. Even better yet, if a person returns to help others.

This ministry is one of leading through serving others. The keys to success consist of listening to and understanding the people I will serve, followed by a genuine desire to help them. I am not a liberal do-gooder who gives away money and things, then feels good about it and moves on, actually deluding myself into believing that my actions have changed someone's life. I mix a pat on the back with a kick in the butt, each when appropriate. Over the course of my life, I have learned that other people are almost always smarter than you initially believe, but perhaps not always in the exact way that you might guess. For example, some of the people I have served may not be math or financial geniuses, but they can be far more perceptive than I would have thought. They may not read books well, but they possess keen insight into people and situations. How I act will speak greater volumes than what I say.

I am a strong pro-life advocate. How we treat those in our society who cannot defend or speak for themselves is the mark of our values. Pro-life is not exclusively about the abortion and euthanasia issues, but encompasses everything in between conception and natural death, including areas such as support for the poor and struggling families with young children, advocating for the physically and mentally disabled, and proper care for the elderly and more.

I have found that in order to capture the attention and earn the trust of a person who needs help, it is necessary to treat him or her with the dignity of being a unique person who is created in the image and likeness of God. I must realize that everyone I meet can do something better than I can. Can I patiently probe long enough to help them find it? Can this effort inspire them to greater confidence and build hope? These are real challenges.

Leadership in the classical Roman style is a top-down model. Since many down the chain of command will only respond to direct orders, this type of leadership stifles ingenuity and promotes laziness. It also puts undue burden, responsibility and pressure on the leader. Real leadership is being a good example and supplying the people you lead with the resources they need to excel. As a deacon, I try to minister in a way in which I do not micromanage.

The book *Heroic Leadership: Best Practices from a 450-Year-Old Company That Changed the World*, by Chris Lowney, helped me to understand better, reorganize, and take to a new level many concepts I practice in my life of service. Harry Truman described leadership as "the art of persuading people to do what they should have done in the first place" (Lowney 15). This approach is also the art of proper marketing and sales (I can relate very well to the Jesuit philosophy, because, essentially, the Jesuit influence and education in high school and college informed and shaped me as I grew up. My father died when I was three, my mother worked six days a week as a telephone operator, and we lived with my grandmother. The Jesuit philosophy and culture was my primary male influence.). I have incorporated into my ministry the following four values or pillars of success that have served the Jesuits well in their ministries (Lowney 9).

Self-awareness: I need to have an understanding of who I am and an awareness of my strengths and weaknesses. I may not be someone who emotes empathy and feeling, nor be the best person to plan liturgical services, because I do not consider attention to detail one of my strengths. In those cases when I must do those things that are not in my bag of talents, I find someone else who has those strengths and let them serve as my guide. When I can, I compensate for my weaknesses, however, with my strengths. For example, I may not know the right words to say to a person who needs comfort, but I do have the ability to listen and give credence to the other person's feelings. Mainly, self-awareness inspires me to discover, through prayers and the input of others, who I am. Once I do, I rely on God to work through me to say the right words. (Don't worry when you are brought before others in My name, I will give you the right words; paraphrase of Mark 13:9–11.)

Ingenuity: Once a person knows himself or herself, it is much easier to become comfortable with ingenuity. A person gains security by knowing rules and regulations, such as commandments, laws, and doctrine, and then discovers where there is flexibility. I can help people focus on what is really important so that they do not feel intimidated by rules and procedures. To me, this ministry requires a solid theological base in order to help people achieve balance. Experience and maturity are the great teachers. I am not sure where I heard this quotation, but I have found that it synopsizes the idea: "The young man knows the rules; the old man knows the exceptions." A healing ministry does not consist of administering the same treatment to everyone and expecting a cure.

Love: As one of my foundations, I utilize "Love one another as I have loved you." If I can demonstrate love by becoming a small beacon of God's immense and unconditional love, I can help people overcome their fears. FEAR can lead to *F*orget *E*verything *A*nd *R*un. Fear and love cannot coexist for any length of time. I seek to help people change this attitude to *F*ace *E*verything *A*nd *R*ecover. Many times another person has difficulty facing fear alone. If I have love, the people whom I minister to in times of crisis will sense that they are not alone.

Heroism: I believe that heroism means not being afraid to take action. In order to affect change, someone has to take the lead. Initiative and disregard for the stigma that might accompany being in the minority are important traits of someone who practices heroism. Another aspect of heroism is to do what needs to be done and not to be concerned about who gets the credit. I have learned through participating in team sports that individual "stardom" alone does not make for a winning team. We must each do our part and be satisfied if the game is won. A hero does not lay blame on someone else if there is a setback; instead, a hero is secure enough to take the responsibility.

I strive that my ministry be based on service that is undertaken with love, joy and enthusiasm. The springboard to freedom is acceptance and forgiveness. I see too many people who practice their religion in a *FOG: F*ear, *O*bligation and *G*uilt. For example, if a person attends Mass on Sunday only because he or she has been told that missing Mass earns a person a ticket to Hell, they are likely to find it meaningless. If they do not attend, they may suffer fear and guilt. What a trap they find themselves in! Jesus was not a technocrat! As a matter of fact, the one group of people that bothered Him most were the technocratic Pharisees and Sadducees. Effective ministry helps people in a way that avoids leading them into a quicksand of guilt.

Those who wish to effectively minister to others should not feel afraid to share their humanness, including their mistakes and weaknesses, with others. Instead of preaching, I share my life experiences, and often the people whom I minister can identify with this approach because they realize that difficulties are a part of every person's life. They can then take what fits them at that time in their lives and leave the rest. This approach is not intimidating or blaming, and it is more likely to give comfort and greater understanding to the person who is in crisis.

One of the gifts I have been blessed with is the ability to organize well. People are sometimes overwhelmed by a problem and cannot see a solution or a way out. I help by showing them how to break the problem into smaller, more manageable pieces. I also help them understand a logical progression and what is their role in this process. I have seen many people try to help loved ones who have personal or faith-based problems. Unfortunately, sometimes the people who try to help someone approach the situation by providing an answer to fix the person or problem, rather than help guide them through a growing process. As a deacon who is relatively quiet and non-imposing, I help people organize a plan and point them in the right direction so that they can begin to address their issues. Ministry success can frequently best be measured, not so much as by how well we attain our own goals, but rather by the growth of those we have touched.

The ideals in my ministry are not wholly founded in religious doctrine or Scripture, but rather practically blended with personal experience and divine guidance. Today, about 70% of the people who identify themselves as Catholics do not attend Sunday Mass with any regularity. Piously talking to them about the Magisterium or papal decrees is probably not going to change their habits. I believe that anyone who answers God's call to service needs to be able to reach people on their level first, before we can expect to show them how having an intimate relationship with God can be invigorating and meaningful. As ministers, we need to meet people where they are, without condemnation or complication. If we stand on the other side of the bridge and yell over to them that, "It's great over here in religionville" and expect them to walk over to us, our approach is bound to produce very little success. We need to be able to walk over to their side, talk to them and then walk back over the bridge with them, hand in hand.

BIBLIOGRAPHY

Lowney, Chris. *Heroic Leadership: Best Practices from a 450-Year-Old Company That Changed the World*. Chicago: Loyola Press, 2005.

*Deacon Peter and Cathy Falkenhausen
St. John the Evangelist Catholic Church, Valdosta*

Peter Falkenhausen

I AM CALLED BY God to serve. On the surface, this statement seems simple enough to be the foundation on which I do what I do every day. The process of building on this foundation, which is Christ centered (1 Cor 3:10), has been a journey, however, that I am still traveling. Along this journey, I have experienced times of enlightenment, discernment, challenge, debate, sharing, celebration, and love. This life expedition has navigated me through courses in theology, spirituality, history, and ministry. I have only begun to scratch the surface of what there is to know about the relationship between God and man. To borrow a phrase from former

Secretary of Defense Donald Rumsfeld, "There are things we know that we know. There are known unknowns. That is to say there are things that we now know we don't know. But there are also unknown unknowns. There are things we don't know we don't know." I will try my best here to articulate what my current "knowns" in the area of theology and spirituality are as they apply to my ministry. I am still a work in progress, but are not all of us at some point in our lives? So, we are at least where we are in life at this very moment, and so at this point is where I shall begin.

When God calls the prophet Jeremiah, He says, "Before I formed you in the womb I knew you, before you were born I dedicated you, a prophet to the nations I appointed you" (Jer 1:5). The narratives of the Old Testament reveal that the Providence of God is accomplished through men and women, chosen by Him, to act in the world. There are no biblical narratives in which a specific person(s) whom God calls rejects His invitation openly and continue their life as it was. No one in the Bible says, "Lord, find another person, because I like life as it is and do not see things changing just because you picked me." Now, there are plenty of examples of weak people who at first doubted God's choice of them or who eventually fell short because of sin. There are those people who failed to listen to prophets and to know God's will for them. A direct and personal refusal of God's call to service, however, does not seem to make the pages. Yes, one could say the people as a tribe or nation refused to obey but I refer specifically to the individual. Again, one might be inclined to point to Jonah, who tries to run from God's will (John 1:10), but God's persistence causes Jonah to comply (John 3:3).

How many people simply never acknowledged God's invitation and, consequently, their story is not joined with God's? One can assume that thousands, like today, failed to realize God's call because they simply did not hear, pay attention, or perhaps were ignorant of His presence. Maybe they feared what might become of their lives. Acting upon God's call to service is a life-changing event. Courage, wisdom and trust can be found in the response to God's call in the stories of Abraham, Moses, Samuel, Isaiah, and especially Mary. At the Annunciation, Mary, who even though "troubled" by the angel's message, agrees to bear a child, knowing the pregnancy will be viewed as scandalous. She knew her life was about to change radically, but she trusted in God enough to be His handmaid. For me, Mary's calling is a reminder that God called me to be a part of what He is doing. Whatever He leads me to do in my ministry will require me at times to act outside of my comfort zone and challenge me to have trust in Him. The vocation of deacon will be at times countercultural. Listening and discerning God's call is not something I can ignore, however, and I want my life story to be a positive part of God's plan in the world. I want people to experience their own relationship with the Lord and just being a part of that process is awesome beyond words.

When Elijah fled to Horeb and hid in a cave (1 Kgs 19:11–18), it was not in the strong wind, earthquake, or fire, but in the "tiny whispering sound" that he heard the Lord speak to him. We should not expect the clouds to part and the angels to sing just before God tells us what he wants of us. Some might want this very direct and up front communication, but if God called us so aggressively, would our actions occur out of a loving relationship with Him or out of fear? Would we have the faith to trust Him as Mary did? Like in the whisper that Elijah heard, do we take time to find God in the everyday life events? I am learning to take time out of the day to reflect on where I encountered God's goodness and blessings, and I try to discern how these encounters reveal His plans and desires. I also reflect on where I may have failed and need to work. This reflection often involves thinking about the people whom I came in contact with this day, the people I may have avoided, or the sudden unexpected events that occurred. I try to focus on what I learned about the people I met. What did they say? What did I say or promise? In what state were they when we parted ways? What did I learn about me? As a deacon, I am called to serve God's people and His Church. I need to be attentive and encouraging; after all, they are my brothers and sisters in Christ. I realize I will not be and cannot be their savior, but I can help them know Christ better if my actions and attitude are Christ-centered. I have learned that we are not meant to make this journey alone, and so I want to pass on the wisdom of knowing that none of us are alone in the walk or the struggle. My ministry centers upon the needs of people who may be looking for guidance, basic survival needs, or a ways to serve God, the Church, and His people.

I too have needs that I cannot ignore, but I know already that they are often met through being part of the activities in my community, Church, and the lives of other people. Sometimes, I may be no more than the conduit to introduce one person to another for something much greater in the future, and not even know at the time it was God's will for them to meet. Sometimes, I will turn to others for guidance and assistance with a situation. I feel I must be among people, for I find God at work most often in peoples' lives. I am by nature very much an extrovert, but I appreciate the strength displayed by people who are contemplative and introverted. I am aware that everyone possesses different God-given gifts and that it is acceptable not to be strong in all things. I used to think there was something wrong with me, but I understand better now how each person has his or her own unique gifts and each of us is capable of using them to serve God. I will always pray for the people I meet along my journey, and I wonder what God calls them to be and to do.

I knew a young Air Force Reserve chaplain (Catholic priest) who often spoke of two experiences that he had. One experience was a visitation when he was younger, and the other was a Eucharistic miracle event while he was in seminary. The first experience had to do with a beautiful woman (he assumed the Virgin Mary) dressed in white with a white rose who visited him in his room and foretold of his future priesthood. Eventually, he began to follow the writings and direction of people like St. Louis de Montfort, who focused their lives on Marian spirituality. The second experience occurred at Mass while he was in seminary. He, in addition to other people at Mass with him, saw rays of colored light emanate from the host when the celebrant held it up at the consecration. Since I had read stories of similar miraculous events, I did not have serious doubts about what he had told me. After a while, though, I wondered if he began to doubt what he had seen. Often, while celebrating Mass, he elevated the host very slowly while staring at it intently as if he expected something to happen. After holding the host high, a bit longer than the length of time priests generally do so, a sense of disappointment could be seen on his face sometimes as he lowered the host to the altar. This priest searched for extraordinary confirmation of his calling to serve God. Yet, the miracle he hoped to see never materialized, and, consequently, in the process, he momentarily forgot about the grace he received at ordination and the sacramental nature of his priesthood. His intense search for extraordinary confirmation did not allow him to see the everyday miracles that occur in the presence of other people, especially the people who are most in need of help.

As a minister and a person called by God to serve Him, I aspire to be Christ-centered by allowing myself to be conformed to His image. I gain much confidence in knowing that God is on my side: "We know that all things work for good for those who love God, who are called according to his purpose. For those he foreknew he also predestined to be conformed to the image of his Son, so that he might be the firstborn among many brothers. And those he predestined he also called; and those he called he also justified; and those he justified he also glorified" (Rom 8:28-30). God wants me to succeed when I serve Him. It is easy to blame God when we experience difficulties, but, in reality, there must be something else wrong: "Whoever is not with me is against me, and whoever does not gather with me scatters" (Matt 12:30). God does not work against Himself, so there must be another explanation for problems. It is important to have the confidence that prayer will lead to the realization of the presence of God. The Spirit may help by revealing a solution, the cause, or another purpose. I gain confidence in knowing that the Holy Spirit will guide me as long as I am willing to turn my life over to God. While I may be on the wrong path, I know that help is not far away as long as my heart is open to God's love and mercy. God's intervention may come in the form of an unexpected event, or it may be a visitor who possesses the wisdom to solve my problem. I am not looking for extraordinary miracles; instead, the everyday experience that God shares with us in the lives, and especially the gifts, of other people have the same impact as miracles. We must remember to turn our lives over to God: "If God is for us who can be against us" (Rom 8:31b). In addition, the words of Julian of Norwich are comforting: "every kind of thing will be well" (*Julian of Norwich* 229).

While I have strived to be Christ-centered, I have been challenged to change my view of how I see people. Admittedly, I have years of stereotypes, prejudices, and cultural bias with which I must constantly fight in order to embrace all my brothers and sisters. The most difficult challenge has been in the conflict between my patriotic ideology and universal social justice. I know there is a desire in me to preserve the standard of life that I believe offers my children the best opportunities to be successful. I realize that people who have been given much are expected to utilize what they have for the good of others (Parable of the Talents, Matt 25:14-30).

How am I to embrace God's children on the one hand and, on the other hand, calm the fear of people who feel threatened, often by the people I seek to embrace? The question is relevant to the immigrant population, primarily Mexicans, in Georgia. Fortunately, my pastor lived in South America and has extensive experience working with migrant farm workers in Georgia. I depend upon him for guidance. Since there is no sense in reinventing the wheel, ministers should be willing to consult with people who have faced the same challenges. I am comforted in knowing that I have deacon brothers from whom I can speak with about the challenges of my ministries. When I minister, I look for the root of the problem, because often overt issues mask a more serious situation. I feel the Holy Spirit leads me to people who face serious economic hardships. Many immigrants, primarily Mexicans, leave Mexico in search of a better life and risk their lives to do so. It is not wrong to want to feed, shelter, and care for your family, and I know I would do the same if I lived in a country whose government failed to provide for its people. I advocate for policies that will change the conditions that leave a country's citizens with no choice but to immigrate. My message to the people, like Hispanics, who feel threatened in the United States is to read the words "In God We Trust" on the currency, encouraging them not to forget that God guided the Founding Fathers. As to calming the fears of those who feel threatened, I will tell them to look at the dollar and remember that it is in God that our Founding Fathers claimed to have trusted, not gold, land, health care, education systems, etc. If people feel threatened by the presence of immigrants in the United States, perhaps they should take a more active stance against the conditions that drove them to the United States. The last thing we should do is blame the powerless. It is much easier to criticize a situation while enjoying a latte than becoming engaged in understanding the depth of a problem and finding a solution.

As a Catholic, it is easy to pick a side of the abortion issue. Most practicing Christians do not advocate for abortion outright. It is in the nuances of conditions or allowances where divisions occur. The subject of right to life, especially in the case of the death penalty, incites a variety of reactions and emotions among Christians, including Catholics. A local Baptist minister commented about the debates during the 2008 presidential election. The topic about which the minister spoke was how one Republican candidate, Mike Huckabee, could have responded, if time had permitted, better to the CNN YouTube Debate question, "What would Jesus do about the death penalty?" The minister took the position that Jesus lived among us as a redeemer, drawing on the biblical account of the adulterous woman. The minister continued by noting that Jesus was not here as a priest to judge, but He will fulfill that role after the Resurrection. The host of the show and the minister referred to St. Paul, explaining that Paul advocated that Christians should abide by local authority and comply with the laws. As Christians, they said, we are here to save souls, but the government has to ensure public safety by enforcing laws. I believe that Christians should participate in prison ministries to save souls, because everyone should have the opportunity to know Jesus; judgment and mercy is the domain of the states, courts, and elected officials to decide. I agree that St. Paul did encourage people to comply with their respective governments; he was not going to advocate rebellion. The radio show failed to address a fundamental question: Why in the modern age, in a predominantly Christian country with vast technological advances, do we in the United States still feel that a person is enough of a threat, even after being captured, found guilty and imprisoned, to warrant the death penalty?

I am concerned about innocent people who have been wrongly convicted, but I am also concerned about those who are guilty. Millions of dollars are spent on the seemingly endless litigation of cases of people who are sentenced to death, who, after many appeals, are still guilty. Why not only one appeal unless new evidence appears that could exonerate them? Meanwhile, they serve out their natural life in prison. Modern technology can prevent people from escaping. The truly guilty owe society for the gift they wrongly or mistakenly take from it by killing another person. There should be a way for death-row inmates to return something to society. Yes, there are those inmates who should never see the light of day, and I am not against making life hard on them. Killing a killer is more often about an eye for an eye, and it sends a message that not all life is sacred. Ground is lost when allowances are made, including war, which is why the military tool should only be used to keep evil in check before the innocent are harmed.

Why not have someone spend the rest of his or her natural life in prison? Does it cost more than all the money wasted on appeals? In the end, the guilty die, and did they have a chance to change who they were before they died? As a Christian country, we should give them as many years as it takes to change. I know that people can and do experience conversion of heart before their sentence is carried out, but what about true healing? Do they get the chance to heal from the life-long circumstance that led to the tragic actions that incarcerated them? Most killers do not wake up one day and decide to be pure evil. Most do not lead normal healthy lives either because of their own poor choices, lack of skills, or the sins of others in their past. I do not want to forget about their victims and those people who were left behind to mourn, but killing the killer does not bring true relief. Forgiveness, however, can work miracles. For example, the actions of the Amish community in Lancaster, PA, which, after the tragic murder of their children, while in school, reached out to the murder's family in their loss, too. There, in these people of simple living, was the active Gospel message of the cross. Out of horrific loss, they found strength not in revenge or retaliation, but in the embrace of forgiveness—they found solace with God.

There are many challenges like the ones I have mentioned that I deal with in my ministry. Over the past several years, God, working through many mentors, directors, and teachers, has formed me and given me great gifts from which I draw. I am not alone, and I am not singularly responsible for anyone's salvation; we have but one savior, and that is Christ. I know that I am not gifted in all things and that there are many people with God-given talents to help build up the Church. As a deacon, I am led by the Spirit to recognize and empower others to use their talents. All is gift, and people should be encouraged and given the opportunity to reflect the light of Christ in their special way. I feel very blessed to be able to be in a position where I can help people come to know they are loved and gifted. It is a privilege to watch them shine. I know I will be faced with people who are experiencing sadness, anger, and loss, but I realize that in all things I will find God. I am very open to Ignatian Spirituality, and I plan to study and exercise this view of living in God's world—it fits me like a glove. I still have so much more to learn, but I am ready to put what I do know, my "knowns," into action. It is time to learn from experience, and it is time to minister in God's on-the-job training camp: the Parish. I leave open, then, the idea that I will become wiser, or in time more, more knowledgeable about what God is doing in the world.

BIBLIOGRAPHY

Julian of Norwich: Showings. Translated, with an Introduction, by Edmund Colledge, O.S.A. and James Walsh, S.J. Mahwah, NJ: Paulist Press, 1978.

Rumsfeld, Donald. "N.A.T.O. Press Conference." Brussels. 6 June 2002. Online: http://www.nato.int/docu/speech/2002/s020606g.htm.

The Spiritual Exercises of Saint Ignatius. Translated, with a Commentary, by George E. Ganss, S.J. Chicago: Loyola Press, 1992.

Deacon Richard and Yvonne Halbur
St. Stephen, First Martyr Catholic Church, Hinesville

Richard Halbur

I FOUND MY CONNECTION with our Lord and Savior through daily prayer, devotion to the Eucharist and continual meditation, asking for His wisdom and to do His will, about challenges and difficulties.

I come from a financially poor background but a strong spiritual family that prepared me to handle challenges by teaching me that the Lord does not let us down. If you ask for His forgiveness, thank him for His graces, and make an effort to do His will, God will provide for our needs. God pours out many graces and blessings upon us, and we must not only be receptive of the blessings, but we must thank Him as well.

God blesses us in many ways. When the Lord pours out His blessings, like rain, upon us, we can either hold a bucket upright, at an angle, or sit on it. If we hold our bucket at an angle, the bucket will not fill up; if we are not receptive to God's blessings, we can rest by sitting on the bucket. When we hold the bucket upright, however, it fills up. Like that bucket, we must be disposed to receiving God's blessings.

My experiences throughout life have continually prepared me for the journey I began when I answered God's call to be a deacon. I grew up in the Midwest as a farmer's son, working the fields, caring for livestock and learning to build whatever was needed for shelter. In spite of the death of my grandparents and other loved ones, including a brother whom I was very close to, I remained faithful to our Lord. I served in the military, raising a family of three children with my wife, who is continually teaching me with the Lord how to love. My time in the military provided me with opportunities to travel the world and to meet many people from a variety of backgrounds. This experience helped me to understand different cultures, and I feel blessed to have had this opportunity.

I had the misfortune of going to Desert Shield and Desert Storm in 1990 and 1991 to assist in the liberation of Kuwait. My time in the Middle East has been a traumatic issue for me and many others who have seen firsthand the casualties of combat. Prior to my combat experience, I always had strong faith in God. While I was in the Middle East, however, I experienced with respect to my faith the saying, "You do not know what you have until you lose it." Before I deployed, I learned that I was not allowed to take my Bible, but I did. I was able to attend Mass only two times in seven months. Consequently, I prayed and read the Bible on a daily basis. When I saw non-Christians stop whatever they were doing and pray, I decided I would pray to God, and the time I did each day helped me keep my sanity. The Lord has given me the strength to deal with many horrific experiences, both at home and in the Middle East. He blessed me with the peace to prevent a soldier from killing a commanding officer and with the courage to drive a burning fuel truck away from a field hospital to prevent it from exploding, which would have resulted in many casualties. Last, but not least, I prayed continually that all of our soldiers would return home safely, and for their families. Seeing the casualties of war, friend or foe, the ugliness it does to one, and the hurt it causes to families, is very humbling. The wives and mothers holding the bodies of their loved ones, crying as our Blessed Mother cried for her son at His torture and crucifixion.

These feelings, sights, sounds and smells stay with you the rest of your life, and sometimes they come back to haunt you in the night. All you can do is ask the Lord to help you overcome and continue to serve Him. As a result of my experiences, I feel that the Lord is calling me to minister to soldiers and their families. I pray that I can be there for them whenever they need to talk, hold a hand or receive a hug. Not only do I want to be there for them to provide comfort, but I also want to give the Eucharist so that they can experience peace of mind. I want to let them know that it is possible to live with these demons, but it is necessary to stay prayerful and to count the many blessings that all of us have, which include, especially, the freedom to pray and receive the sacraments. We can rebuild our lives slowly and share God's blessings with our spouses and families so that we can serve God. When two or more people are gathered in God's name, all things are possible: "If your brother sins, go and tell him his fault between you and him alone. If he listens to you, you have won over your brother." "Amen, I say to you, whatever you bind on earth shall be bound in heaven, and whatever you loose on earth shall be loosed in heaven. Again, Amen I say to you, if two of you agree on earth about anything for which they are to pray, it shall be granted to them by my heavenly Father. For where two or three are gathered together in my name, there I am in the midst of them" (Matt 18:15, 18–20).

I also have been given the gift of organization. Consequently, my parish relies on me to handle many different responsibilities. It is important that a parish not depend on one person, however, to do the things that need to be done. It is not always easy to find people who are willing to share the responsibilities. All of us, however, are called to answer the Lord's call in one way or another. We all need to work for the Lord so that we can continue to grow in His love and share with the rest of the world our joy and love of the Eucharist. If we use our gifts with those of our friends and community, we can all work together to do God's will and bring peace to many people. I feel called to help people, but especially my fellow soldiers. I want to serve them and our Lord by sharing my love of the Lord and His Body and Blood toward the attainment of everlasting life in heaven with our Heavenly Father. With God's guidance, I know I can answer the call to minister to men and women soldiers who suffer to this day from the horrors of Vietnam and more recent wars. I view my ministry as providing comfort and counseling so that they will recover physically and spiritually.

I close my essay with a passage from Sirach that speaks, I believe, to all people who hear God's call: "Some he blesses and makes great, some he sanctifies and draws to himself. Others he curses and brings low, and expels them from their place. Like clay in the hands of the potter, to be molded according to his pleasure, So are men in the hands of their Creator, to be assigned by him their function. As evil contrasts with good, and death with life, so are sinners in contrast with the just; See now all the works of the Most High: they come in pairs, the one the opposite of the other. Now I am the last to keep vigil, like a gleaner after the vintage; Since by the Lord's Blessing I have made progress till like a vintager I have filled my winepress, I would inform you that not for myself only have I toiled, but every seeker after wisdom" (Sir 33:12–18). Amen!!!

*Deacon Dave and Cathy Hayden
St. Michael Catholic Church, Tybee Island*

Dave Hayden

As I reflect upon the transformation I have undergone since I answered God's call to serve Him, I realize that I am able to appreciate the connection between my spirituality and the study of theology. The understanding of theology that I gained provided me with the knowledge that I, and anyone who seeks a deeper relationship with God, must be willing and able to grow spiritually. In 1 Corinthians 15:57–58, we read about victories in the name of God, but no victory is ever won without true spirituality. Spiritually-informed and -shaped victories lead to an abundant life with Jesus Christ. A healthy spirituality allows us to face all of our difficulties and to be able to serve others fully. In addition, a healthy spirituality provides us with the comfort of knowing that true victory is wherever God is.

I have experienced several of these victories since I said, "Yes" to God. My victories include an understanding of my spirituality and how to nurture it. I do not see spirituality as the magical solution to all of life's problems. I am not a person who is unwilling to face his problems or weaknesses; I accept my weaknesses as a part of who I am. I accept the imperfections and flaws of my humanity, however, as enlightening and redemptive. My spirituality is not one that depends upon God to do everything for me. I do not employ rituals, like attending Mass on Sunday, as a means to create a sense of security. A healthy spirituality does not make an idol out of religious symbols, objects, or practices. It requires a foundation of personal honesty, based on self-knowledge, self-acceptance, and a willingness to accept reality. My spirituality is filled with compassion, openness, and respect for others; it enables me to enjoy warm, loving relationships. My spirituality does not allow me to be isolated from other people, and it accepts everyone as a child of God.

My new-found spirituality has given me a renewed passion for life, the result of which is a better prayer life and compassionate action for peace and justice. I recognize that honesty with oneself is a core value of life; consequently, I am committed to regular self-examination. Furthermore, I understand that pain and failure can lead to a deeper spirituality and appreciation of who we are as sons and daughters of God. I recognize what is the truth and stand for it with passion.

The journey to discovering one's spirituality is more special if it is shared with another person, such as a spiritual guide or a mentor. The feedback that a person with experience can offer is invaluable to the direction of this journey toward a greater appreciation of God's presence in the life of each one of us. In addition, the shared journey promotes growth of the individual on the journey, as well as the growth of the person or people who share the journey. Frank Sinatra's famous line "I did it my way" is a risky mantra for the person who seeks a more profound relationship with God. We are communal people who need to share and to challenge each other in order to discover our strengths and weaknesses.

I owe my spiritual self-discovery, in large part, to the courage God gave me to share my journey with other people. Each of us, as unique and special in God's eyes, can learn from one another, and our individual stories are capable of helping other people discover their God-given gifts. In the presence of people who share intimate details of their relationship with God, the feelings of vulnerability that we experience can have a positive impact on our own journey. When other people share their experiences with us, and we, in turn, open up to them, we learn to listen to and to respect other people; in addition, we gain a greater understanding and appreciation of our own relationship with God.

There are so many Catholics today who are hungry to find God in church. I imagine there are an equal number of people who seek the religious tradition that practices the spirituality that is best for them. As disciples of Jesus, how can we feed the people who experience spiritual hunger? We can do so with the ingredients of the Bread of God: hope, compassion, mercy, understanding, and, most important of all, love.

Like Jesus in His day, we are called to reach out to the people of our time who find themselves marginalized from the Church by their own beliefs or from society for any reason. Jesus dined with the Pharisees and debated the meaning of the Torah, Prophets and Psalms with them, as well as with other religious leaders of His time. He ministered to those Jews who simply were not able, for whatever reason, to connect to the Judaism of their time. In addition, He ministered to people who were not Jewish. Likewise, we are called to *minister* to all people by bringing God to them.

The call for leadership is a call from God, and we must be aware and sensitive to this call. In order to be effective leaders, though, we must devote some quiet time to Him and to hear Him when He speaks to us. We cannot be leaders unless we listen to God, and we cannot listen to God unless we are still. We will only be able to appreciate His awesome presence in our lives and to feel Him tug at our hearts if the time we spend in prayer is quality time. If we practice a devoted prayer life, we will hear God's call to leadership. A call from God is different from other calls, because we can be sure it is the right one. When we begin to doubt the wisdom of the calling, we hesitate to answer it, or, and much worse, we reject it.

We must remember that when God calls us to lead, He will equip us with what we need to be successful. All of the men and women He called were ordinary people like each of us. If we answer God's call, He will transform our limitations and weaknesses into life-changing qualities.

We cannot say that we have little to offer to God, because He is capable of moving us in ways we cannot begin to imagine.

As servant leaders, we are to be the living embodiment of the life of Jesus. We must learn, therefore, how to live as God's servants. One important step toward this goal is letting go and letting God. Our primary concern should be to do whatever God asks of us and to be ready to answer His call to serve others. There is a natural desire to limit our social circle to people who are like us, but we must fight against this desire by reaching out to help wherever and whenever we can. As we enter into a deeper relationship with God, we are able to recognize where He wants us to be as ministers. As servant leaders, we are to foster in each other attitudes of gratefulness for what He has done, and we should have confidence in what God will do in and through our lives. God's love for each one of us is capable of inspiring us to serve in His name.

During His ministry, Christ emphasized often the many virtues of love, honesty, justice, diligence, actively caring for others, and reconciliation. Furthermore, Christ made it clear that the relationship with one's neighbors was the key sign of the health of one's relationship with God. In a world plagued by discord and war, societies today need the reconciliation that only Christ can offer. I believe that a vision of Christ's reconciliation is the most important gift that Christians can give to the world. Indeed, the ultimate reconciliation between God and His people is already under way. God, who is *not* responsible for the problem, assumes the burden of pain that discord creates and loves it into wholeness.

Most non-Catholics who seek to enter the Church find the Sacrament of Reconciliation a bit troubling. Couples who participate in the marriage preparation program often say that there is no transgression for which they could not forgive their future spouse, but they do not seem to understand that the Sacrament of Reconciliation is a much deeper experience than forgiveness alone. Words such as *confession*, *repentance*, *forgiveness*, *restoration*, and *reconciliation* are connected to the Sacrament. God forgives the sinner who repents, and He removes the burden of guilt. Any harm caused by the sin can be restored to wholeness through actions that are uplifting and empowering. Subsequently, a new relationship can begin on a firmer and more truthful footing.

Recognition of how a sin affects a person and the way he or she behaves is necessary to answer the call to turn away from sin. This endeavor can only come to fruition, however, through true repentance. God wants us to ask for forgiveness, but reconciliation does not come easily. It requires a psychological, personal, and spiritual commitment to the way that Jesus lived His life. Since Christ took the sins of the world upon Himself, each one of us must take responsibility for our own sins, and this step is only possible if we possess a true recognition and understanding of who we are as sons and daughters of God and the nature of our spirituality so that we can nurture it in our lives.

Deacon Bob and Cathy Kepshire
St. Teresa of Avila Catholic Church, Grovetown

Bob Kepshire

"**T**HEN I HEARD THE voice of the Lord saying, 'Whom shall I send? Who will go for us?' 'Here I am;' I said; 'send me!'"(Isa 6:8). My call to the diaconate was not as profound as that of Isaiah, because it was revealed to me over a period of several years. At the time, I did not know in what direction the Holy Spirit was leading me. I was only aware that my spiritual life was in the process of being reborn. The experiences of watching my mother take on the Cross while she battled ovarian cancer, and my subsequent spiritual experience at the moment of her death, were precursors to my spiritual awakening. As my interest in Benedictine spirituality grew, so did my ability to be open to the voice of God. I believe that this happened as a result of my practice of *Lectio Divina*, as well as praying the Liturgy of the Hours. It is hard to describe, but I just knew that God had something in mind for me. I had a purpose to serve the people of God in ways beyond my vocation as a nurse. So, in the summer of 2003 I found myself assembled with twenty-eight other men of varying backgrounds and positions along the spiritual continuum to begin the discernment process toward ordination to the Permanent Diaconate. Five years later, I was one of twenty-two remaining candidates in our final preparations before we entered Holy Orders. What a journey! What a privilege to be here. The purpose of this essay is to reflect on my journey. In addition, I will articulate my personal spirituality and theology of diaconal ministry and how I see myself serving as an ordained minister of the Roman Catholic Church.

The Aspirancy Year (first year) was by far the most powerful portion of the formation process. I believe that I was able to learn more about myself as a person as a result of living through the Aspirancy Year than through any other situation I had ever experienced in my life. Furthermore, I was able to experience a whole new relationship with God. I found that the Retreat in Everyday Life and the Spiritual Exercises of St. Ignatius of Loyola were very powerful experiences. The following passage is from a paper that I had written during the Aspirancy Year:

> I was never in the military, but looking back on the experience of the Aspirancy Year/Spiritual Exercises, I think it would be safe to say that it was like spiritual boot camp. You take a group of guys with different backgrounds and ideas, yet all of whom want to achieve the same goal. They are then exposed to something they have probably never experienced before: they are removed from their comfort zones and challenged to think outside of the box. They are all then given a uniform approach (the Spiritual Exercises) to help to mold them into soldiers for Christ. The idea is not to break the person down, but rather to lift him up, allowing him to bloom spiritually. The Exercises took me through a personal Paschal Mystery. I found that I struggled with the process at first, because I felt beat up with all of the emotions that accompanied the process; at one point, I "died," because of a feeling that I was not going to succeed. I questioned whether I thought I could be a deacon. But, the resurrection did come! That "ah-hah!" That empowering feeling that God was calling me! Even with all my faults, God called me. God was not looking for perfection—He was looking for me, as I searched for Him.

As this realization became my own reality, I felt at peace and affirmed with the thought of becoming a deacon. When we discussed in one class the concept of "Deus Semper Major" (God who is always more/greater), I felt that the entire discernment process was greater than me. My life experiences took me along a path to push open the door that God had unlocked. He had always been there waiting for me to come by and visit, and He knew I would do so in my own human time. I like to fish, so here is an angler's take on it: God goes slow trolling with a big hook and enticing bait. Sometimes the waters are rough and the fish go deep, but God, being a good fisherman, keeps on trolling, knowing the holes the fish like to frequent. He allows the fish (us) to taste the bait and even to play with it, and when the time is right, he sets the hook deep and reels in the catch! But unlike an angler who hopes to have a big fish fry, God allows the fish He catches to make an individual choice if they want to come on board the boat.

I believe that we all have a calling of one sort or another. We all have a purpose on earth to serve God in some fashion. For some of us, it is a call to ministry, be it lay or ordained. If someone were to ask me twenty years ago if I was going to be ordained some day, I would have answered with an emphatic, "I doubt it!" But, God obviously had a plan for me. I firmly believe that my entire life's experiences were a preparation that brought me to this point. When the call came, it was with a good bit of trepidation that I proceeded with the application process. There was an inner voice that kept telling me it was the right thing to do, while I kept questioning if I had the "right stuff" to become a deacon. The Aspirancy Year helped me to sort out my feelings and to realize that the inner voice I was hearing was the Holy Spirit, guiding me along this new and unchartered path that was to become part of my spiritual journey.

The Aspirancy Year opened my eyes to see that God accepts me as I am. My entire notion of sin, punishment, worthiness, etc. was transformed. I firmly believe that we all punish ourselves much more harshly than God ever will. I believe that God is a spiritual force so grounded in love that it will be us who will choose our ultimate fates, for if it were up to God, we would all live in paradise. God gives us a free will to do as we choose here on earth; it stands to reason that we will also have that very free will, therefore, when the time comes for our spirits to leave these earthly vessels. The power behind this belief is that it should give us great consolation to know that God loves us infinitely. Through the Aspirancy

Year, I learned to accept this love from God. Instead of doubting myself or thinking that I am not worthy, I came to understand that all is a gift from God and that I truly am made in God's image. I came to realize that it is perfectly acceptable to try to be all that I can be. Through the teachings of St. Ignatius of Loyola, I learned that I need to use all of my talents (gifts from God) to their fullest; in that way I am praising what God has done for me.

The Aspirancy Year also gave me the courage to address some deep wounds that I had been carrying inside of me for a long time. I believe that going through the Retreat of Everyday Life and developing my spirituality helped me to understand who I am as a person. It was a very holistic experience. That first year developed our spirits, our hearts, our psyches and our personalities, and we were challenged to be open to other ways of experiencing the love and graces of God. We were introduced to new notions about who we were as disciples and encouraged to develop lasting and loving relationships with our brother aspirants. In addition, we developed an understanding that it is acceptable to love ourselves, to take care of ourselves and to nurture ourselves. Through these realizations, I was able to understand what has caused me pain throughout my adult life, and why I have feared being a failure in life. What is more important, I now know that I am not a failure. I am aware that I have done much good and have been successful; perhaps most important of all, I have so much more to offer God's world. The Aspirancy Year gave me the tools that I needed to progress through the rest of the formation process. I will never forget that year of my life.

The last paragraph from the Prologue of the *Rule of Saint Benedict* states:

> Truly as we advance in this way of life and faith, our hearts open wide, and we run with unspeakable sweetness of love on the path of God's commandments, so that, never departing from his guidance, but preserving in his teaching in the monastery (diaconal formation) until death, we may by patience participate in the passion of Christ; that we may deserve also to be partakers in his kingdom. Amen (11).

I believe that the formation program was just the beginning, as I anticipate life-long formation as a deacon. With that said, I would like to reflect on my educational formation. Where do I begin? I can only say that it has been quite a journey! The educational requirements have been a challenge, because we had to balance the class demands with family and work. I experienced, however, a strong inner drive to keep pushing forward. There were many times that I felt overwhelmed with trying to finish my reading assignments, my WebCT postings, the essays and other assignments. I sacrificed my spare time and did so without any animosity. What drove me to give it the best that I could? I believe it was inspiration from the Holy Spirit. I embraced God's call with my entire being, and, consequently, I found the time and the energy to complete my studies.

Every course was special in its own way. I can honestly say that I enjoyed every class, and, more importantly, I learned a great deal in each of them. The striking aspect for me was that with every bit of new information I gained, I came to realize how much I really do not know. I am much better informed than I was when I began, but now I embrace the reality that I will remain a student for the rest of my life. It is both sobering and also invigorating. My realization is sobering because I thought by the age of fifty, I could retire from being a student; it is invigorating, because I know that I will continue to be challenged and have the energy to pursue more knowledge. This perspective, I believe, will only serve to make me a better servant to God's people and also to help to continue to grow even closer to God.

The courses on the Hebrew and Christian Scriptures were excellent, and I believe they were a very solid introduction to biblical research and interpretation. I really enjoyed the courses on the History of Christianity and Spirituality as well. I think it was important to learn about our roots and how the Church has progressed through the ages—knowing where we came from will only help us to better understand where we are headed. Learning about the various spiritualities (Ignatian, Franciscan, Benedictine, etc.) was especially moving to me. I can see a little of each in me. The course work on Theology was extremely informative, as was our in-depth review and study of the documents of the Second Vatican Council. I think we have been well prepared to answer questions regarding our faith and will be able to do so with a sense of confidence.

As with the Aspirancy Year, our educational formation was extremely invaluable. We were blessed with some exceptional instructors, and we have been exposed to a wide variety of topics and information. But, as I grew in knowledge with each passing course and year, I can say that I experienced personal growth as well. I am not the same person I was when I started the formation program. I appreciate much more the simple things in life, and I see God in so many different ways now: I see Him in nature, in people, and in myself. My mind has been opened to knowledge, and my heart and spirit have been opened to the wonders of God. I see the face of Christ in so many more situations than I ever did before, and I am so thankful to have a new perspective of the world. How much more peaceful and content I have become. I feel that God is working in and through me, and I have become an instrument to do His work here on earth.

During the entire formation program, I discerned if serving God as a deacon was my calling. Time and time again, I asked myself, "Why me? What have I done to be singled out for this vocation?" In the beginning, it was a mystery to me, but as time passed by, I discerned why I have been called. I can relate well to Mark 1:16-20, The Call of the First Disciples:

> As he passed by the Sea of Galilee, he saw Simon and his brother Andrew casting their nets into the sea; they were fishermen. Jesus said to them, 'Come after me, and I will make you fishers of men.' Then they abandoned their nets and followed him. He walked along a little farther and saw James, the son of Zebedee, and his brother John. They too were in a boat mending their nets. Then he called them. So they left their father Zebedee in the boat along with the hired men and followed him.

I, like the disciples Jesus called, am an ordinary guy. I come from a blue-collar background, and I live a rather uneventful life. I never sought fame or attention, and I have dedicated myself to providing for my family by working hard and trying to be the best at what I do. I am not a saint; I have my faults, and they are many. Like the first disciples, though, I have had some worldly experiences (street smarts). I do not think God was looking for extraordinary men when He called me and my brother deacons. I believe He sought ordinary men who were willing to embark on an extraordinary journey. During the Aspirancy Year, I learned how to appreciate my gifts in order to serve God more effectively. God called me for various reasons: I have the ability to listen to people and meet them where they are at; I have the gift of a quick wit, and I can make people laugh; I have a big heart and can empathize and cry with another person when he or she is suffering; I have walked the same confusing path as most people do, and I have stumbled and become lost along the way, too. I do not know what the journey will hold for me in the future, but I place my trust in God and allow the Holy Spirit to be my guide.

I feel that Martha and Mary in the following passage from Luke embody the spirituality of diaconal ministry:

> Jesus entered a village where a woman named Martha welcomed him to her home. She had a sister named Mary, who seated herself at the Lord's feet and listened to his teachings. Martha, who was busy with all the details of hospitality, came to Jesus and said: Lord, is it of no concern to you that my sister has left me all alone to serve? Tell her to help me. Martha, Martha, you are anxious and upset about many things; one thing is only necessary. Mary has chosen the better portion, and she shall not be deprived of it (Luke 10:38–42).

Mary represents the contemplative approach to diaconal spirituality, which consists of listening to the Lord in personal solitude and reflecting on His word (*Lectio Divina*). Martha represents an Ignatian side to diaconal spirituality, as she was "doing," putting her faith into action. She was able to express herself not only spiritually, but also physically and intellectually. Is either approach better than the other? I would have to say, "No," as one could be effective spiritually using either form. To be a deacon, however, one needs to possess a balance of both Martha and Mary. As a deacon, I need to be Mary—prayerful, at peace and one with the Lord. I need to listen to His word, and, as Mary, I must always be a student of the Lord. I need to be Martha too. I must be eager to perform service to the Lord and His people. In addition, I must pay attention to the details and work hard, even when my work appears not to be appreciated.

There needs to be a balance in my approach to diaconal spirituality and my vocation as a deacon. Each approach will support the other. When it seems like the service I perform is without rewards, I depend upon prayer for strength and guidance. Then, I put the prayer into action through service to others.

I believe the passage I cited from Luke also represents the "liturgical" side of being a deacon. Mary represents the Liturgy of the Word, because it is important to be attentive and to contemplate what the Word says and how it is a call to service. Martha, "who was busy with all the details of hospitality," represents the Liturgy of the Eucharist. The story of Martha and Mary is, on the surface, simple to understand, yet the underlying message is deep and powerful.

My attraction to Benedictine spirituality is also tied into the role of a deacon. The Benedictine maxim, "Ora et Labora" (Prayer and Work) relates closely to the Gospel story of Martha and Mary. As a deacon, my spirituality finds strength through a strong and devoted prayer life. I enjoy praying the Divine Office because it helps me to feel close to my confreres at Saint Meinrad Archabbey. The Divine Office is also the prayer of the Church, and I find spiritual strength in the knowledge that clergy and religious throughout the entire world pray the Office. I believe that my practice of *Lectio Divina* assists me in preparing to proclaim the Gospel at the liturgy, in addition to when I am called to preach. When I listen to the Word of God through meditative and contemplative prayer, I am able to hear and to feel when God speaks. The guidance of the Holy Spirit provides me with the insight to help other people understand the Gospel and discover ways to apply it to their lives.

The "Labora," or work, is the *diakonia*, or service, which is the real heart and calling of a deacon. The work can be classified into three categories: 1) spiritual work; 2) liturgical work; and 3) social work. I believe to be spiritual, one has to work at it. It is not some sort of miracle that takes place. Spirituality has to become part of who you are, and it takes discipline and purposeful action. Due to the various demands placed upon us on a daily basis, the decline or loss of a spiritual side of ourselves is a real threat. As a deacon, I aspire to maintain balance in my life, and, in order to do so, I nurture my spiritual life, my family life, my professional life and my clerical life. Each of my "lives" is inter-related because each realm makes up who I am. An essential aspect of the balance I seek is scheduling activities that recharge my batteries, because I know that I have to do activities that energize me and provide me with a fresh perspective on my life. If I do not do these activities and break away from my routine, I can lose focus and risk experiencing burnout.

Each of the spiritual traditions we studied during the formation program has strengths and attributes that can benefit anyone who answers God's call to service. Though I may lean towards the Benedictine tradition, I value and admire each of the other spiritual forms we have studied. I think it is wise to learn about the different spiritualities in order to be prepared more fully for the challenges of ministerial service. For example, when working with the poor, a Mendicant or Franciscan approach is very valuable. The focus of these two spiritualities is the specific spiritual needs of the people who need guidance and assistance.

Benedictine spirituality is rooted in community. This mode encourages each member of the community to use their talents for the good of all. Additionally, there is a strong prayer life of embracing Scripture (via the practice of *Lectio Divina* and the importance of praying the Divine Office in order to recognize the holiness of everyday life). Benedictines also have a commitment to hospitality; they accept strangers as if they were Christ (*Rule of St. Benedict*, Chapter 53). This way of life, consisting of devotion to prayer, desire to work, and openness to reach out to strangers, reflects what God expects from us as His sons and daughters. A strong prayer life is essential to guide each one of us on our journey of service to God and His Church.

Ignatian spirituality, in my opinion, is the best of both worlds (Benedictine and Mendicant). The Jesuits have a sense of community among their members, and their focus is on service to others. The major strength of Ignatian spirituality, I believe, is its active nature. There is an overwhelming mode to be proactive, to identify what needs to be accomplished, and to go out into the world and do God's work. Of the three spiritual models that have been discussed so far, the Ignatian approach is much more modeled, in my opinion, after the way Jesus carried out His ministry. Jesus was the Incarnation, and St. Ignatius' approach consisted of seeing the Incarnation in the world around him. Based upon His ministry to people, Jesus truly was the first deacon. I personify Ignatian spirituality by modeling my diaconal ministry after how Christ served others and following His deep embrace of living a spiritual life.

For me, there is no set formula to diaconal spirituality. Each deacon, or anyone who wishes to serve God, can aspire to follow one of the great spiritual traditions, but, in the end, the tradition chosen will only serve as tools to support what we define as our own individual spiritual tradition. Every deacon must indentify his own spiritual rhythm and define how he will live a spiritual life.

According to the *Catechism of the Catholic Church*, the deacon "shares in Christ's mission" in his ministry:

> Deacons share in Christ's mission and grace in a special way. The sacrament of Holy Orders marks them with an imprint ['character'] which cannot be removed and which configures them to Christ, who made himself the 'deacon' or servant of all. Among other tasks, it is the task of deacons to assist the bishop and priests in the celebration of the divine mysteries, above all the Eucharist, in distribution of Holy Communion, in assisting at and blessing marriages, in the proclamation of the Gospel and preaching, in

presiding over funerals, and in dedicating themselves to various ministries of charity (392–93).

This description of the duties of a deacon would seem to focus heavily on the deacon's liturgical roles. The "various ministries of charity" are very important as well. Service to God's people is the core of being a deacon, and it consists of the meeting people where they are in life. This aspect of *diakonia* is the one that I am still discerning. The social service aspects of my calling are a bit daunting, given the complexity and grave state of social issues we are faced with in our world today. As deacons, we will have a foot in two worlds: the world of the hierarchy of the Church as a clergyman, and the world of the laity, living a life deeply connected to the trials and tribulations of everyday life. Due to this unique perspective, we are well suited to see and experience the realities of trying to live as Christians in a world that all too often is far removed from any semblance of faith or spirituality. It is vital that every deacon, therefore, has a theology of ministry to help guide his work in Christ's vineyard.

There are three foundations upon which I will build my theology of diaconal ministry:

1. Christology—based on the writings of Karl Rahner
2. Church as Community
3. Servant Leadership

According to John P. Galvin, the foundation of Rahner's Christology centers upon three theological themes: "[. . .] God's universal salvific will; Jesus' indispensable role in the mediation of salvation; and the completeness of Jesus' humanity" (316). Karl Rahner has deep convictions regarding the salvific will of God. This will is extended to all humans, from those who lived before the time of Christ to the present day, including the people, who through no fault of their own, have never had the opportunity to hear the Good News of Jesus Christ. In what seems to be in conflict with the teaching of God's universal salvific will, Rahner also holds that Jesus is an indispensible mediator of salvation. Finally, Rahner relates that there is much misunderstanding on what the Church actually teaches regarding the divinity and humanity of Jesus. To address the misunderstanding, "[. . .] Rahner developed a conception of Jesus as the definitive Savior, or the eschatological [final] Mediator of salvation" (Galvin 317).

Rahner stresses that Jesus exercised his human freedom, but at his death and Resurrection, his divinity was fully manifested. Rahner's theology of Christology, to me, is so important to diaconal ministry. Jesus was simultaneously man and God. He did not turn these two aspects of himself off and on depending on the situation. His humanity and divinity were the essence of who Jesus was and still is. As deacons, we, too, find ourselves living within two realms. We are ordained clergy, as well as men of the world. We have expectations placed on us based on our clerical state, while, at the same time, we have to provide for our families and continue in our secular professional endeavors. Additionally, we cannot turn our diaconal attributes off and on depending on the situation. We are always deacons and, as such, must act accordingly.

In addition to the personal ties to Rahner's teaching of Christology, his teachings are a solid foundation upon which to base a theology of diaconal ministry. Rahner's approach to Christology fully embraces the Paschal Mystery. The Paschal Mystery is the essence of Christianity, and, therefore, it must be at the heart of the theology of diaconal ministry. As deacons, we must be willing to carry Christ's Cross. Furthermore, we must be willing to die onto ourselves and find new and everlasting life in following the way of Jesus the Christ. Our lives should be a living and visible sacrifice to others that should act as a beacon for others to follow. We need to be able to help others along their individual journeys as they carry the Cross. In addition, we should be able to help people to understand that the Paschal Mystery is alive today in them, as it was in Christ, and that as we celebrate the Eucharist, it not only is the real presence of Christ, but It is an affirmation that we, too, will travel the same journey as Christ.

Another key component of my theology of diaconal ministry is the concept of Church as community. According to the *Catechism of the Catholic Church*, "In Christian usage, the word "Church" has three inseparable meanings: the People that God gathers in the whole world; the particular or local church [diocese]; and the liturgical [above all Eucharistic] assembly" (871). The universal nature of the Church is so powerful, and it causes me to reflect on how great God is. From a theology of diaconal ministry, this notion of Church as community helps to lift up the universality of the Catholic Church. It also is a reflection of the ministry of the deacon.

When we approach ministry from a universal view, it really takes in the communal aspects of the role of the deacon. The diaconate is an order of service, and the deacon, ever mindful of the world, especially all of its needs (spiritual, physical, psychological, and material), the deacon must respond accordingly to offer support and assistance. In spite of the large net that a deacon should cast, he is not called to have expertise or the ability to be all things to all people. Rather, he must be aware of his unique strengths (gifts), strive to develop them and put them to good use to serve others.

Probably one of the most visible and public aspects of diaconal ministry is how we relate to the local community and our liturgical service. The relationship that many people have with a deacon, and, for that matter, the priest, is limited to Mass and other liturgical celebrations. It is important that deacons, therefore, exercise their liturgical roles with reverence. When we, as deacons, serve at the altar in a reverent and dignified manner, come well prepared to proclaim the Gospel and, when appropriate, preach in a manner that helps to connect the significance of the Word of God to the lives of the people, we represent the role of the deacon in a very positive and meaningful way.

In addition to the liturgical aspects, the deacon's ability to become connected to the local parish or diocese through participation in a variety of ways is a major component of diaconal ministry. There are many opportunities to serve, including visiting the sick, counseling couples who are struggling with their marriages, taking Communion to the homebound, providing adult educational sessions, and administering the appropriate Sacraments. The deacon has the ability to demonstrate in many ways his call to service.

Servant leadership is the essence of diaconal ministry. According to Michael Kwatera:

> The deacon and the assembly are 'made for each other,' in the sense that his service to them should deepen their sense of being the Body of Christ, while their service to him should deepen his sense of being a fellow member of that Body. Every special liturgical ministry [including that of priest and deacon] exists for the sake of the primary minister, the assembly [not vice versa]; the priest and deacon share the unique ministry of coordinating the other ministries for the full and active participation of all the members of Christ's Body (22).

As deacons, we must take the servant leadership role to other people. A servant leader is a person who seeks no material or personal reward. We are to serve with a sense of humility that reflects God's calling to do His work.

There is a song that we sing every Sunday at our 9:30 am Mass to send off the pre-school children to their Liturgy of the Word. It is called *I Want to Walk as a Child of the Light*, by Kathleen Thomerson:

> I want to walk as a child of the light. I want to follow Jesus. God set stars to give light to the world. The star of my life is Jesus. In Him there is no darkness at all. The night and the day are both alike. The lamb is the Light of the city of God. Shine in my heart Lord Jesus.

This song is so simple, but yet so very powerful, and it gives me such a sense of peace when I hear the words. I think it holds a special message for me as I continue my journey of sacrifice and service to God. Since I answered God's call to serve Him, I was privileged to have some wonderful professors who opened my mind and heart in ways that I never thought possible. I made life-long friendships, and I feel that I am part of something so much bigger than myself. I pray that I will find the grace, through the guidance of the Holy Spirit, to live my ministry in a manner that serves God and His people to my fullest ability. I believe that God will continue to shape my personal spirituality and theology of diaconal ministry. I also believe that the gifts I receive from others will also help to shape my ministry. I know that no matter where God leads me lead, I will always have a light to guide me along the way.

BIBLIOGRAPHY

Catechism of the Catholic Church. 2nd ed. Washington, DC: United States Catholic Conference, Inc., 1994.

Dysinger, L. *The Rule of Saint Benedict, Latin & English*. Trabuco Canyon, CA: Source Books, 1997.

Galvin, John P. "Jesus Christ." *Systematic Theology: Roman Catholic Perspectives*. Vol. 1. Eds. Francis S.Fiorenza and John P. Galvin. Minneapolis, MN: Fortress Press, 1991.

Kwatera, Michael. *The Liturgical Ministry of Deacons*. Collegeville, MN: Liturgical Press, 2005.

The Catholic Study Bible. Eds. Donald Senior and John J. Collins. New York: Oxford University Press (U.S.A.), 1990.

Thomerson, Kathleen. "I Want to Walk as a Child of the Light," 1970. No pages. Online: http.//www.sheetmusicplus.com/pages.

Deacon Ken and Patty Maleck
St. Mary on the Hill Catholic Church, Augusta

Ken Maleck

THE ROOTS AND ORIGINS of my spiritual faith journey, as well as the path I have traveled, amaze me as I reflect on it. The fact that the Lord has led me in this direction is beyond my understanding. The exercise in writing of this journey, has, in itself, been valuable for my spiritual development. Thus, this reflection of my first experience of whom God was, seeing from where I have come and how I have grown and matured, is integral to my relationship with Him.

The earliest recollection I have of anything of a religious nature is in my middle school years; I have no recollection whatsoever of my baptism (infancy) or confirmation (fifth or sixth grade). I vividly remember being an altar server during middle school, and I recall being enthusiastic about saying aloud the Mass responses in Latin. I felt as though I was participating in the Mass by doing so. Also, the server's role during the offertory and of holding the paten during Communion gave me a felt sense of being an integral part of the Mass.

I really had no sense of spirituality, however, in those formative years. As this time period was prior to Vatican II, spirituality was for priests and bishops. People in the pews were there to listen and understand as much as possible the Latin Mass. There wasn't much of a heartfelt sense of God's presence in our lives, or even in the Church, for that matter. The pre-Vatican II Catholic was a worshiper whose spirituality consisted primarily of obedience to rules. One had the sense that God was watching from a distance, keeping a checklist of what you did wrong. This concept of God quickly led me to the "guilt trip" syndrome, where I basically felt guilty most of the time for even the slightest transgression. This, in turn, I believe, resulted in a poor self-image and lack of confidence in me.

This absence of spirituality and mistaken concept of God's roles in our lives did not cultivate a happy childhood. It was difficult for me to receive the sacrament of reconciliation. I was always extremely nervous and fearful of the outcome. I never warmed up to the concept. Perhaps, my discomfort was due to not knowing that God had forgiven my sins already. In addition, I wish I had known about the parable of The Prodigal Son—that very warm, inviting image of the father running to meet the son as the son is running home to his father. Like the father, God always welcomes us home, regardless of what we do.

Efforts to understand more about my Catholic faith did not bring me any closer to God or to an understanding about my faith. My biggest source of frustration in those early years was not being able to get anything out of the Mass. If the Latin Mass was not a big enough obstacle, the sermon, read in either Slovak at my church or in Polish at my grandmother's church was. Still, I was nonetheless influenced by my religious experiences during this time of my life. I firmly believed in God, the Trinity, and what the Church represented. I was constantly searching for more, but never finding it.

As my concept of God was evolving, becoming more and more concrete, a number of events helped to shape it. While working a summer job with a tree service, I was assigned to work with a young seminarian, Joe Mack. One day, we were planting shrubs at the Carmelite Monastery, where the nuns lived in a cloister (prohibited from having outside contacts). It was my first visit to the monastery since I had gone with my grandmother years ago to bring food donations to the nuns there. As we worked planting the shrubs, I began to think about the calling the nuns must have to be contemplative to such a degree to live in a cloister. I asked the seminarian why they chose this vocation instead of another, more visible ministry. He paused for a long time, and then replied, "So they can be closer to God." It was the first time I heard that phrase, and it remained with me, giving me more inspiration for thought.

Life away at college marked a trend away from the Church. I began freshman year attending Mass regularly, but by the time winter arrived, the twenty-minute walk from campus to the church was too uninviting. When I returned home for summers and vacations, I attended Mass at my mother's insistence, but at college I went only occasionally, when the Spirit moved me. In senior year, a new energetic priest celebrated Mass at the campus chapel, and I began to attend more regularly with more of a focus upon the homilies (which were on current topics) than the Eucharist and what It could do for me.

Because I did not have a relationship with God, I found myself doing unexplained actions for no apparent reason. At one of the Masses on campus, the usher asked me to bring up the Gifts, and I refused. Perhaps it was my immaturity, but it continues to trouble me that I did that. I was still searching but not getting anywhere. It was not until many years later that I came to realize that all the qualities and characteristics, either inherited or shaped in these formative years, were chosen by God for me. Once I realized that my early religious experiences, as troubling as some of them were, had a purpose, I became mature enough to praise and thank God for them.

Two significant turning points in my relationship with God, who He is and how He makes his presence known to us, occurred in my mid-twenties. It was during these events that I felt God's presence. I sensed that He was inviting me to a new relationship, asking me what was going on in my life. The first occurred in May 1976, alongside my close friend, Dennis Adrat. He was twenty-seven, married, and with two toddlers. He had fought off Hodgkin's disease for six years, but, now, he was losing the battle. I visited him frequently. On one occasion, he seemed particularly depressed, knowing that his final days were drawing near. I asked him if the priest had been in to offer him the Eucharist, and he immediately rebuked me. He became incensed, leaned over, stared at me directly in my eyes, and said sternly, "If there was a God, a person in my situation wouldn't be suffering through this." I was completely taken aback and dumbfounded. I felt as though an arrow had pierced my heart. He continued staring at me, expecting an answer that would comfort him. To my amazement, I came up empty. Nothing came out. Dozens of thoughts ran through my head at warp speed, and I knew there was a solid faith-based answer for him, but for the life of me, I could not think of it. As my heart slowly returned to its normal pulse, I felt God saying, "What is your faith life all about?" and "Am I close to you two guys?"

I had never been so disappointed in myself, as I could not comfort my close friend in a time of need. The episode affected me on a deeper level, though. It occurred to me that I had been a checklist Catholic my entire life; my faith life had no meaning. For the first time in my life, I asked myself where I was going with my faith life. Would I ever get close enough to God to answer questions like Dennis'? Had I ever asked the same questions of myself? I walked away from the hospital that evening a bewildered person, asking myself what God was all about. Dennis passed away a few weeks later.

The day I married is the second turning point in my spiritual life. On that glorious, warm spring day, I found a new life, new hope, and a renewed sense of purpose. I still vividly remember that day some twenty-seven years ago. For the first time in my life, I experienced the joy of the power of the Holy Spirit. I felt such a heightened state of happiness that I wanted to rejoice. During the Mass, I became conscious of the fact that that three of us, not two, were participants in this event. God, in the form of the Holy Spirit was right there, actively working to provide a covenantal relationship between the three of us. Although this concept was alien to me at that moment, I distinctly felt as though nothing I had ever done previously in my life could begin to compare to what I was about to undertake. More importantly, I felt that God had a hand in doing it.

My wife, Patty, has been the most influential person in my spiritual life. Her relationship with God was firmly established at the time I met her, and I was fortunate enough, through the workings of the Holy Spirit, to allow her to positively influence me. She has been my mentor on this journey, and without her, I would not have pursued a deep commitment and relationship with God, prayer, and the Church. She has been a guiding light, never pressuring me, but, rather, allowing the Spirit to work at whatever pace God deemed necessary. This process took place over a number of years.

As I returned to the Church, I gradually took on a more active, participatory role. Upon moving to Georgia in 1981, I felt the longing to be a lector. The pastor warmly welcomed me, and I soon sensed that the spoken Word of God became meaningful. I was not just reading a fairy tale or a bedtime story; I was speaking with a sense of urgency that God was calling each one of us to a life with Him. Lectoring on Holy Saturday and during the Confirmation liturgy are times when I most feel the presence of the Holy Spirit. When I read aloud the words from Ezekiel 36:26, "I will give you a new heart, and place a new spirit within you, replacing your stony hearts with natural hearts," I can hear God asking me to shed my stony, callous temperament and replace it with a kind, loving one. My twenty years as a lector has deepened my understanding of the importance and relevance of the proclaimed Word of God.

A few years later, I began to see the value in serving others. My life was not all about me, but it actively involved others, helping where I could, where my talents were of use. Serving others became a gift, not a chore to be done grudgingly.

Over a period of eighteen years, my attitude toward small faith-group sharing programs changed dramatically. Upon joining a "Heart Renewed" program in 1986, I begrudgingly participated, finding little of value it in for me. But something kept calling me back to these groups. A few years later, I tried it again, and I warmed up slightly to it. A few years later, through the workings of the Holy Spirit, I became a small group facilitator for the "Disciples in Mission" program. I found myself looking forward to participating in these group sessions, even more so in the last five years. They have resulted in a renewed prayer life and an awareness of the burdens and "crucifixions" of others. The other participants have taught me that God is near—a companion on the everyday journey.

Being a religious education teacher has enhanced my faith life as well. For seven years, I experienced firsthand the meaning and value of communicating God's plan to children who have doubts, misconceptions and suspicions at a critical time in their intellectual and spiritual formation.

I feel as though all these events have brought me closer to God, deepening my relationship with Him. The same feeling intensified when I entered the diaconate formation program. I soon discovered that one does not develop a deep sense of spirituality until one sees God as loving, caring, and actively working in us at all times. The Trinity is with us on our everyday journeys, according to Hugo Rahner, S.J., providing the fervent hope that all of our life's experiences will bring us closer to God: "Go with us on our everyday roads that these too, may be paths which lead into your kingdom, for it is in sober faithfulness in everyday things which brings us wisdom and maturity." Praying these words from Rahner help me appreciate how God truly is in all things, and finding Him there is what the focus of life should be.

My faith life grew leaps and bounds throughout the formation program and continues to do so to this day. When I pray at Perpetual Adoration, I no longer find myself thoughtlessly reciting the rosary. Rather, I feel as though I am there to talk to God one-on-one, as a loving friend. It is the real me with the real God, discussing all the trials and tribulations of everyday life. In spite of all our weaknesses, God loves us just the way we are, and He wants to hear all about it. Another difference I have noticed in myself is that when I see people of an alternate sexual orientation, I no longer cast aspersions on them. Rather, I find myself saying, "God loves them just as much as He loves you, Ken."

I have become more acutely aware of God's love for me and for the people around me. I discovered that all of the qualities of who I am about which I felt most proud are gifts from God, who loves me exactly as I am. Thankfully, God is not finished with me yet. Never before had I thought that God continues to dream and have great hopes for me. I am confident that He will reveal to me His plan, as long as I invite God into my life and establish a relationship with Him. God calls me to serve Him in new ways. I pray that God will continue to bless me with the many rewards that await me underneath the challenges, tribulations, and life experiences I am sure to encounter because I said "Yes" to God.

BIBLIOGRAPHY

Rahner, Hugo, S. J. "The Prayer of the Apostles." *Magnificat* (February 2004): 83.

Deacon Michael and Leticia McGrath
St. Matthew Catholic Church, Statesboro

Michael J. McGrath

WHEN I BEGAN THE Permanent Diaconate formation program in the fall of 2003, I had no idea that my life would undergo such drastic transformations. I entered the program because of a passionate desire to answer God's call to serve Him. I have since come to appreciate more fully the fact that God is alive and active in everything and everyone around me. Consequently, I welcome each day of my life with enthusiasm for the possible ways in which I can serve God, and I long to discover the holiness of everyday life and to help others realize how God is present in their lives as well. My personal transformation began when I answered God's call, and my theological and spiritual development continues to open my eyes to the many ways in which God is present in our world

My knowledge of the theology and spirituality of ministry began to develop during the Aspirancy Year of the formation program. Ignatian spirituality, especially its focus upon finding God in all things (F.G.I.A.T.) and the spiritual process of outer→inner→outer, has had a big impact upon my spiritual life. While I always believed that God was responsible for the world in which we live, I had never truly appreciated to what extent until I began to study Ignatian spirituality. I discovered how to appreciate God's omnipresence and to see how the laboring God continues to walk with each of us on a daily basis. The book *Moment by Moment* contributed greatly to my spiritual growth and my knowledge of theology during the first year of the program. The exercises included in this book informed and shaped my spirituality, and they also provided me with the opportunity to learn more about the relationship between theology and spirituality.

The material I studied in the classes I took to fulfill the requirements of the Master of Arts degree in Pastoral Studies not only contributed greatly to my knowledge of the Bible, but it also inspired me to learn more about the Word of God. God speaks to us in so many different ways in the Bible, and I believe that it is incumbent upon every Christian to share God's words of healing, compassion, and love with others.

My relationship with God and the Church was, for the most part, restricted to my interior life. Even though I felt called to serve God, I never understood how and to what extent until I began the formation program. When I answered God's call to ministry, I affirmed my desire to serve *both* Him *and* the Church:

> Intrinsically linked to the sacramental nature of ecclesial ministry is *its character as service*. Entirely dependent on Christ who gives mission and authority, ministers are truly "slaves of Christ," in the image of him who freely took "the form of a slave" for us. Because the word and grace of which t hey are ministers are not their own, but are given to them by Christ for the sake of others, they must freely become the slaves of all (*Catechism* 232).

I aspire to be an effective universal servant of ministry so that I may make possible God's universal call to holiness. When I said, "Yes" to God's call, great things happened in my life, and I want others to experience the same joy and passion I now feel for service to God.

When I reframe my earliest exposure to Spanish (classes, study abroad) against the backdrop of what I have done with the language and the decisions I have made, I am convinced that my call to serve God began long before the day I decided to apply to the diaconate formation program. Today, in addition to my apostolate to the English-speaking community of my parish, I feel blessed to be able to minister to our Spanish-speaking brothers and sisters. Furthermore, my vocation to minister to prisoners and to the elderly who are in nursing homes inspires me to communicate to both populations that the Paschal Mystery is happening now for everyone and that their curent surroundings do not define them or their relationship with God. It concerns me, however, that many shut-ins experience desolation, which St. Ignatius defines as "obtuseness of soul, turmoil within it, an impulsive motion toward low and earthly things, or disquiet from various agitations and temptations. These move one toward lack of faith and leave one without hope and without love. One is completely listless, tepid, and unhappy, and feels separated from our Creator and Lord" (*The Spiritual Exercises* 122). In spite of their circumstances, prisoners and the elderly should be encouraged to find consolation, defined as an "increase in hope, faith, and charity, and every interior joy which calls and attracts one toward heavenly things and to the salvation of one's soul, by bringing it tranquillity and peace in its Creator and Lord" (*The Spiritual Exercises* 122). People who experience desolation must realize that any form of spiritual consolation (fervent devotion, intense love, tears) is a gift from God, and in order to resist feelings of desolation, a person should find strength from God through prayer and unwavering faith. My ministry consists of sharing my beliefs that our laboring God is the eternal source of consolation and that all things proceed from Him, who walks with us throughout our spiritual development.

My call to serve God has many goals, but there is one that is the essence of my mission: to empower the people I serve with a belief of acceptance. In order to have a relationship with God, each one of us must accept that God loves us unconditionally and completely. From an early age, we develop a basic trust that someone accepts us as we are. In his book *Young Man Luther*, Erik Erikson addresses the importance of nurturing a trust that someone is there for us:

> Basic trust in mutuality is that original "optimism," that assumption that "somebody is there," without which we cannot live. In situations in which such basic trust cannot develop in early infancy because of a defect in the child or in the maternal environment, children die mentally. They do not respon or learn; they do not assimilate their food and fail to defend themselves against infection, and often they die physically as well as mentally (Van Breemen 2).

As we become older, however, the people on whom we depended, generally our parents, are not as central to our life. Unfortunately, many children grow up with only one parent or, in some cases, another family member in the absence of the biological parents. When our parents or that person who represented the "someone else" we trusted is not a part of our life, where do we find acceptance? The answer is with God.

God accepts each one of us as we are and not as we should be. His love for us is the foundation of our relationship with Him, and the cornerstone of our faith is a realization that God accepts us. According to theologian and philosopher Paul Tillich, faith is "the courage to accept acceptance" (Van Breemen 3). It is not easy, however, to practice faith according to Tillich´s definition, for human nature leads us to doubt that God accepts us as we are. Also, many people base acceptance of themselves on their own qualities, some of which they refuse to accept. The idea that we must mend ourselves before we present the real us to God is a mistake. Too many people are afraid to bring their true sentiments and burdens to the Lord. St. Ignatius encourages us to give ourselves completely to God, who, after all, knows us better than we know ourselves. True acknowledgement of God´s love and acceptance leads to faith and self-acceptance.

As an "eternal now," the Paschal Mystery is an invitation to all of us to rid ourselves of everything that is death-dealing and to surrender to the Mystery by "actively choosing to reach out and look beyond limitations, blocks, and barriers trusting to find new life, new possibilities, new freedom, etc" (*The Spiritual Exercises* 122). St. Paul's philosophy of salvation is especially meaningful to me: "When everything is subjected to him, then the Son himself will [also] be subjected to the one who subjected everything to him, so that God may be all in all" (I Cor. 15:28). St. Paul's position on the role of God in salvation is so fervent that many of his statements in his letters refer to this belief in one way or another. In 2 Corinthians, for example, St. Paul writes: "So whoever is in Christ is a new creation: the old things have passed away; behold new things have come. And all this is from God, who has reconciled us to himself through Christ and given us the ministry of reconciliation [. . .] For our sake he made him to be sin who did not know sin, so that we might become the righteousness of God in him" (2 Cor 5:17–19, 21). St. Paul describes Christ as "the image of God," whose glory appears "on the face of [Jesus] Christ" (2 Cor 4:4 and 6). It is incumbent upon all who answer God's call to service, who join Christ on mission, to help people realize that death is not the final word and that out of death and dying God brings new life and new hope.

One of the most meaningful and powerful lessons I learned that shaped my spirituality can be summarized in one word: courage. My transformation began when I discovered the courage to accept who I am as a son of God, in spite of my personal shortcomings. An integral component of my transformation to accept who I am was the recognition of my weaknesses. Weakness is the bond that links each of us together, and, for this reason, it is vital that we support one another. God's grace becomes manifest when we present to Him the "real me," the sinner. Each one of us needs to know that weakness is an inherent part of the human condition, and, as such, it relates us deeply to one another and profoundly to God. God called me to serve Him in spite of my weaknesses. Since I answered that call, I have grown in many ways, and because of God's grace, I now see myself as a "wounded healer."

God has blessed every one of us with our own unique gifts, which we may or may not perceive. Before I answered God's call, I did not feel that I was particularly special in any way. While I had always achieved success in many endeavors, I also felt that many people achieved equal or greater success, and, therefore, I was similar to others. When I learned to claim the gifts God had given me, my life changed. I began to appreciate my different talents and no longer felt "ordinary." It is no secret that many celebrities are admired for their talents or their good looks. Professional athletes are revered because they can hit over .300 with power, or they can average more than twenty-five points a game while leading their teams to championships. I do not believe that anyone would argue that singers, athletes, and other people who lead high-profile lives possess gifts that enable them to succeed. What about the majority of the people in the world, those of us who are not widely recognized? Do we have gifts? Of course, we do! The Bible contains many passages that allude to our being gift-filled individuals: 1 Corinthians 12, Acts 6, 1 Peter 4:10, Matthew 5, and Romans 5. Like many people, I suppose, I never truly embraced my gifts. I knew I possessed certain talents, but I never considered them gifts from God. As I look back upon the transformation I have undergone and reevaluate what I do on a daily basis, my gifts have become more apparent to me. I have learned to embrace what I feel are my gifts and to take greater pleasure in sharing them with others. Furthermore, I realize now that my reticence to accept my gifts and the praise of others denied God of His glory. I am eager and ready to help other people embrace their gifts so that they, too, can serve God.

My theological and spiritual growth has had a significant impact upon all aspects of my life. In a few words, I believe I am beginning to see my world through the eyes of God. My ministry joins the laboring God, who calls each of us to be the person He wants us to become. I do not know what God's plans are for my ministry, but I do know that I will dedicate my life to discovering God's Individual Particular Will for me. The transformation about which I have written in this essay has only just begun to mold me into the person I pray that I become. The following quotation from St. Ignatius' Spiritual Exercises embodies the essence of how I view my life now and how I encourage the people to whom I minister to see their lives:

> God's love shines down upon me like the light rays from the sun, or God's love is poured forth lavishly like a fountain spilling forth its waters into an unending stream. Just as I see the sun in its rays and the fountain in its waters, so God pours forth a sharing in divine life in all the gifts showered upon me. God's delight and joy is to be with the ones called God's children—to be with me. God cannot do enough to speak out and show love for me—ever calling and inviting me to a fuller and better life, a sharing in divine life (Smith and Merz 91)

I pray that the theology and spirituality of my ministry will continue to fashion me into a minister who is able to lift people up and to love them into wholeness.

BIBLIOGRAPHY

Buckley, Michael J. "Because Beset With Weakness . . ." *To Be A Priest: Perspectives on Vocation and Ordination.* Eds. Robert E. Terwilliger and Urban T. Holmes. New York: Seabury Press, 1975.

Catechism of the Catholic Church. 2nd ed. Washington, DC: United States Catholic Conference, Inc., 1994.

Smith, Carol Ann, S.H.C.J., and Eugene F. Merz, S.J. *Moment by Moment: A Retreat in Everyday Life.* Notre Dame, IN: Ave Maria Press, 2000.

The Catholic Study Bible. Eds. Donald Senior and John J. Collins. New York: Oxford University Press (U.S.A.), 1990.

The Spiritual Exercises of Saint Ignatius. Translated, and with a Commentary, by George E. Ganss, S.J. Chicago: Loyola Press, 1992.

Van Breemen, Peter, S.J. "The Courage to Accept Acceptance." *As Bread is Broken.* Denville, NJ: Dimension Books, Inc., 1974.

Deacon Patrick and Ellen Mongan
Church of the Most Holy Trinity, Augusta

Patrick Mongan

Welcome to the beginning, the middle, and for some the ending capstone course in our personal and ministerial journey to grow as a companion of Jesus and a Servant of the Gospel as a Now Event bringing Real Presence of Christ to an often very secularized world. Yes, we are preparing and have become Sacraments of Christ.

THIS QUOTATION FROM A course syllabus is a powerful description of our journey to become deacons. As I began this essay, I felt the best approach to a "Theology and Spirituality of Ministry" for me would be to highlight how my personal journey has contributed to my ability to minister to others, and then share my thoughts on some of the "circles" of ministry that I see myself being involved in.

How does one summarize a lifetime of learning, growing, suffering, and experiencing life that has influenced my theology and spirituality of ministry in just a few pages? With great difficulty! So, I can only describe small but key portions of my journey. My age and experience have provided me with many tools and abilities to minister to the Body of Christ and be a "sacrament of Christ," even before beginning the diaconal formation. The diaconal formation program, however, was a true capstone for my journey and helped me to realize the many ways in which I have been blessed. Although I had a pretty good knowledge and understanding of the Church prior to diaconal formation, I have gained a much better integration of spirituality and theology so that it is easier to make it both real and available to parishioners. I envision sharing this knowledge during the discussions I lead in the adult education class on Sunday. As we discuss various aspects of the Church, I am able to share what I have learned about Church history, Scripture, other religious views, and theology. In addition, I am hopeful that I can make our discussions relevant to their lives and present them in a way that challenges them while being "life giving."

Although to question our actions, "Is it life-giving or death-dealing?" may seem self-evident, it is a theme that my wife Ellen and I discuss often. It has reinforced in us the need to help people to be "whole," before they can be holy and be all that God wants them to be! We both desire others to be able to see that they are loved by Christ and gifted by Christ so that they can be the strong women and men of Christ that God wants them to become. As a couple, Ellen and I are so thankful for the many blessings bestowed upon us and want to help others share in the joy that comes with a heart full of gratitude for God's mercy and love for us.

Jesus often reached out to people who were suffering interiorly. As a Eucharistic minister, I look at the faces of the people who come forward, and I believe I can see the pain in them and wonder how can I reach them? How can I help to bring joy and hope to their lives? How can I bring them to Jesus or be Jesus to them? If there is one thing I have learned, it is that there are no easy answers to these questions. As I encounter each person, I must rely on the Holy Spirit to guide me so that I might use the gift of discernment in ascertaining what is, and is not, of the Spirit. What will be "life-giving" for this particular individual? What aspects of myself should I let die, or even perhaps "kill?" The result of my discernment is not only a greater and better life for me, but it will also allow me to be more "life-giving" to others.

Although I had experienced Ignatian retreats prior to the diaconal formation, the first year of discernment, and, subsequently, the study of the various spiritual traditions, solidified for me the spiritual tradition that seemed to suit me best. I have experienced "charismatic" prayer meetings, retreats at monasteries, silent retreats, and regimented times for prayer. "Finding God in All Things" resonates with my spirit, and I have come to see it as a way of life that is just as spiritual as the Benedictines, Franciscans, "charismatics" or the cloistered. One way is not better or worse, more important or insignificant—it is just different. Whatever approach to prayer works for a particular deacon or anyone who answers God's call, it is essential that they be prayerful and constantly relating to God, so they can be open to the Holy Spirit's guidance.

The fruit of this understanding is the ability to see that God has many different ways in which He can help individuals grow spiritually. As a minister, I must not try to force "my way" or "the way" upon someone else; I need to be able to help others find their path, and, then, encourage and nourish that path. I may even need to step out of my comfort zone and walk with them part of the way on their journey. The knowledge of the spiritual traditions in our Church and our history will, I hope, enable me to open the richness of our faith to others. I am excited about our faith and try to nurture that excitement in other people as well. I like to tell people whom I minister to that if they are not excited, they should continue to search until they find something in the Church that gives them energy and excitement, because the Church provides so many ways to grow and experience our faith. The Church is full of "pearls" that I certainly continue to discover and will try to help other people discover, too.

The communal nature of the pilgrim journey that all of us, as sons and daughters of God, travels is most evident in my marriage and family, but it also manifests itself in my relationship with my brother deacons. A motto that reminds me of this communal, yet personal, journey is, "Me with We in He." Our class is representative of the diversity in our communities, parishes, and diocese. We are many different personalities and gifts, all striving to follow the call God placed in our hearts. Because we have realized that we have been called by God to serve, we have gained the courage to be witnesses of our faith and to minister to others. Everyone involved with the formation program received the nourishment of Christ's love. Certainly, my experiencing God's love through people (especially my wife and family) and experiences from God in the Sacraments and sacramentals, instilled in me the confidence and trust to be able to take risks. I possess the strength to follow the movements of the Holy Spirit, in spite of the possible negative consequences. We "live" our theology, which in turn is informed and matures with the experiences of our living it out in our daily lives. Our theology and spirituality work together in us constantly to bring about a more abundant life for us and the people around us.

This pilgrim journey creates a very real tension that crystallized in many ways as I read Chris Lowney's book about the Jesuits titled *Heroic Leadership*. The importance of not becoming too attached to this world is a challenge for me, and I suspect, for most of us. In order to continue on my pilgrim journey, I realize that I need to develop a detachment from the world that surrounds me, without, however, forgetting to remain grateful for the many blessings God and the people in my life have provided me. As incarnational beings, all of us desire what the world offers, but, as sons and daughters of God, we should learn how to use what the world provides to serve each other. The Ignatian "Examen" (self-review) allows me to discern my dependence upon the attachments of the world, including status, power, relationships, and material possessions, so that they do not prevent me from following the movements of the Holy Spirit.

During the years of the diaconal formation program, I asked myself, "What makes you good enough to be a deacon?" As I discovered my own gifts and appreciated more fully how much God loves me, I soon stopped asking that question. What Jesus said over 2000 years ago is still true today: "The harvest is abundant but the laborers are few; so ask the master of the harvest to send out laborers for his harvest" (Matt 9:37–39). As I look around our parish, which God has blessed with many faithful Catholics, I must still answer the question about my calling to be a deacon with, "But if not me, then who?" I believe God has blessed me with the gifts, personality, experience and knowledge to serve others effectively. If I were not to accept God's invitation to make who I am available to others as a deacon, I would be demonstrating a less than thankful heart.

So, how should my ministry as a deacon incorporate my spirituality? My goal in ministry as a deacon is to become a full-time minister in the

Church. When I am able to do so, I plan to spend the first year meeting with as many people as possible. This time will be dedicated to discovering the different ministries that exist in the parish, both the recognized and the unrecognized. It will be a time to discover the aspirations of the parishioners, their hurts, their needs and what the Holy Spirit seems to be saying to them. After much thought and prayerful contemplation, I hope to be able to discern my role in the parish and, then, discuss that with the staff and pastor. One of my greatest strengths in ministry is my wife. Although our personalities are very different, we have gained a unity that could only have come from God and the Sacramental nature of our marriage. She has talents and gifts that complement mine, and together we can bring more skills and perspectives to ministry. She and I have the ability to hear the Holy Spirit in ways that the other does not. I try to involve her in many of my activities (including reviewing this essay), and where feasible, I would include her in the various ministries of the parish where we serve.

To contemplate specific roles can be a double edged sword. To plan and to examine how I may best serve the parish and the Church are positive steps, as I prudently use my gifts and experiences to make the assessment. I must also be open to radical ideas and paradigm shifts, however, if that is where the Holy Spirit is leading me. I now possess a much greater appreciation of just how radical Jesus was for the culture in which He grew up. Yes, the spiritual ideas were radical, but the manner in which He lived out His spirituality in the interactions he had with people was also radical. He was counter-cultural in his relationships with the Samaritans, the Pharisees, the sinners, and, most especially, with women. He brought a major paradigm shift to the Jews' understanding of their faith and culture, which many people, if not most, could not accept.

One of the challenges for a deacon is to make the liturgy and the sacraments "real" to the laity. As I administer the sacraments, I believe it is important to do so in a way that is both universal and personal. As I read the Gospel and deliver a homily, how do I make it alive and relevant for the lives of the parishioners? Finally, how do I bring the Gospel each and every day to my relationships with others?

In perhaps a lesser way, it seems to me that the Second Vatican Council was also a paradigm shift that many people accepted, but it also left some people behind (some people by their own choice, but other people appear to have been truly confused by all the changes) as the

Church moved forward. As I understand it, there was a major growth in collegiality between the laity, priests and bishops as a result of Vatican II. Yet, the recent scandals in priestly abuse seem to threaten this collegiality and create barriers between priests and parishioners. I recently read an example of the distortion that has occurred in Church relationships because of the overreaction to this problem. A woman who was attending a workshop on how to relate to children asked what she should do if a child who is crying approaches, but she is the only adult in the room? She was told to go in the opposite direction of the child. How sad! The ministry of deacons, as servants with one foot in church and the other at home with a family, should involve efforts to decrease any barriers there might be between priests and the laity. Deacons, and clergy in general, need to have the courage to take the course of action that leads to healing.

The courage about which I write extends to challenging apostolic authority when it is necessary. I wonder, "How do I respect apostolic authority, yet speak out when I should?" I pray that I have the courage to follow Jesus' example of love and understanding. While remaining humble, how do I confront people whom I believe to be hurtful to other people? How do I avoid scandal? When dealing with such situations, how do I incorporate the love of Christ and make sure that the correction is done out of a love for those harmed and the person who is the cause of the pain (while they are harming others, they are also harming their souls)? I do not think there are easy answers for these questions, but my hope is that the Holy Spirit will provide me with the courage and grace to answer them according to God's will. In spite of the possible consequences, I believe that I will be steadfast in my desire to heal, because I know that Jesus loves me and that He will always breathe life into dire situations.

During the formation program, there were many discussions concerning ways to address the need for diversity in the Church. All Catholics are called to contribute to this goal, but we must be mindful not to sacrifice the strong sense of unity that exists in the Church. Diversity can be problematic, as I have witnessed how it can fracture a community. Clergy and laity need to determine the root of this animosity and to heal the pain by promoting reconciliation, forgiveness, and understanding. Sometimes, people perceive some views as destructive, even when that may not be the intent of the person expressing the view or the belief. I know of situations where different opinions about how to conduct the liturgy fostered division. As a deacon, I will utilize my skills and knowledge to restore "unity in our diversity." Sometimes, this goal will not be possible in spite of everyone's best efforts. At times, prayer (the most important!) may be the only remedy. As a physician, my experience with patients taught me that I must continue to depend upon the Holy Spirit to remain persistent in my efforts to heal, for this endeavor may take years.

In our community, there has been a wonderful tradition of ministering to the poor, the imprisoned, and the disadvantaged. Furthermore, I can see increasing challenges and growth in this ministry. I have a sense that we might be headed for significant economic problems in this country that will strain our ability to minister to the poor, especially the poor who suffer from medical problems. In response to this situation, I am hopeful that I can help people utilize health care resources more wisely. In addition, I will minister to the poor in a way that will allow them to understand their situation better. Although I have served the poor in the area of medical care, I recognize that I need to understand more fully the causes of their problems, and I pray that I can minister to them with compassion in order to preserve their dignity as people created in the image and likeness of God. How do I help people in my parish recognize the call to minister in those areas that God has put upon their hearts? How do I nurture that call and empower the people who respond by saying, "Yes?" Again, no easy task!

For several years, Ellen and I have given presentations on marriage to engaged couples. We lead a team of several presenters, and we both believe our efforts in supporting marriage and family need to increase. Ellen has counseled many women who experience marital problems or are in the midst of a divorce. As a physician, I have seen the emotional, spiritual, and sometimes physical consequences of divorce. Divorce definitely threatens the integrity of the family in our culture, and we must do all we can to help all families, "the little Church", be what God wants them to be: a "garden" that is life-giving and not death-dealing. Both Ellen and I pray for the gift of discernment, because ministry in troubled marriages can easily lead to burn out and take an emotional toll on all who are involved. Both she and I believe we need to be more involved with couples prior to their wedding and to develop ways to encourage married couples, both new and old.

One weakness I have is a lack of experience with the universal Church, even though I attended churches in Germany many years ago. I have certainly read about the struggles of the Church in other parts of the world, but I do not have any first hand experience. I seek to avail myself of the opportunity to visit the Church in other countries, especially those churches with a great deal of poverty and suffering (As I write this paper, I have discussed with a local priest from Africa a summer visit to Tanzania!). I would like to speak with parishioners in those countries so that I can put a face to the struggles that I read about.

A topic near and dear to the late Pope John Paul II was ecumenism. I interacted closely with men and women of other Christian congregations while I was a member of an ecumenical charismatic community. In addition, I have spoken with Hindus and Muslims. As a result of these interactions, I have learned of the wide-spread ignorance of Catholicism and believe one responsibility of a deacon should be to promote ecumenical dialogue and to educate non-Catholics about our beliefs. Probably the place to start is actually with our fellow Catholics (which I am currently doing), because if they truly understand their faith, then they can educate people about Catholicism in the work place, in schools, and even at social functions. We are called to make the "Good News" available to everyone and everywhere.

A troubling trend today is an ever-increasing hostility towards Catholicism, which reinforces the need to be aware of the "signs of the times." The Church has been frequently the victim of significant hostility from various elements throughout history, so I do not want to overstate the problems. There are increasing numbers of reports of attempts to silence the Church and to prevent conversions to the Catholic faith. These have occurred in such diverse places as India and Australia. I do not think anyone who serves God is immune to these challenges to the Church, even in this country. I do not believe everyone is called to be a martyr, but I must ask myself, if the Lord asked me to give my life for the Body of Christ, would I be willing? How do I deal with this issue without being an alarmist and causing more harm than good? Again, history gives us the example of martyrs, in addition to many people who chose to conform to the culture publicly, while nurturing their faith privately. All of us are called to be "martyrs" by suffering in small ways for Jesus and the Body of Christ.

Shortly after the completion of *CyberCulture: New Challenges for Pastoral Ministry,* one of the courses in the diaconal formation program, I discussed with our pastor and fellow parishioners steps we could take to make the Internet a more useful tool for our parish. There is no doubt in my mind that the Internet is a tool that can help both the laity and the clergy glorify the Body of Christ. It certainly can bring the Church community into the homes of the ill, disabled and homebound. In addition, it can be used to communicate the vision the parish has for itself and its role in the larger community. It is a tool that can enhance the communications between the various parish ministries. These possibilities are just a few of the ways in which I hope to explore how this tool can enhance ministry. The Internet challenges us to change our paradigms, which I believe must occur if we are to benefit from its potential.

I recognize that, in spite of my age and many experiences, my pilgrim journey continues on a new and different path. In my career in medicine, I witnessed firsthand the pain and suffering that is all too common in the world. I have had the privilege of sharing in the journey of my patients, and I pray that I have done so in a hopeful and comforting manner. As a deacon, I pray that I will be able to follow God's dream for me, faithfully and in a grace filled manner. I know that God's molding of me is not complete and will continue until the day I die. I have been blessed with many gifts and many wonderful experiences to share with others, and I pray that my ministry will be "life-giving." I have suffered physical and emotional pains that God has transformed into my fervent desire to be compassionate and caring towards others. My hope is that each of us will be able to serve the Church and be the "face of Christ" for the entire world.

BIBLIOGRAPHY

Lowney, Chris. *Heroic Leadership: Best Practices from a 450-Year-Old Company That Changed the World*. Chicago: Loyola Press, 2005.

Deacon Reinaldo and Bessie Morales
St. Joseph Catholic Church, Augusta

Reinaldo Morales

I BEGIN MY SEARCH for words to explain my theology and spirituality with Thomas O'Meara's definition of ministry: "Ministry is not a document or a state, but an action" (153). This statement marks a paradigm change in the Church and Catholic faith. It challenges our theological and spiritual attitude and our imagination. Vatican II is responsible for the increased participation of the laity in ministry. This new paradigm marks the beginning of a new Church model in which all Catholics have many responsibilities.

O'Meara reminds us that the pre-Vatican II Church is quite different from the Church of today: "The idea of a parish that is simply a station for the rapid reception for the sacraments lies thirty years in the past" (12). Reflecting on the first chapter of O'Meara's *Theology of Ministry*, "Ministry: Between Culture and Grace," I find it easy to see how my cultural experiences have influenced my theology. In addition, I recognize how grace of God has affected my ministry (action). Until I sat down to write this essay, the theology and spirituality of my ministry is a topic about which I gave little thought. As I reflected upon my ministry, I discovered that I do shape it by a specific theology and spirituality, and that I have done so for years.

My theology and spirituality is based on the multi-cultural experiences of the intellectual base of systematic theology of the Western world and the Latin American passion for life in liberation theology. Specifically, I take from liberation theology the focus upon the poor and marginalized. I have lived, worked and experienced life in Europe, the Middle East, the United States and Central America, and I am from the Caribbean (Puerto Rico). These experiences have provided me with a wide variety of cultural interaction that is now an integral part of who I am.

When I began to wonder about my theology of ministry, I was unable to put into words its essence. Now, I see my own ministry as making sense of the multi-cultural framework of which I am a member. This multi-cultural vision informs my theology of ministry.

Staring into the logo that represents my ministry, I begin to see the heart of my ministry—action. I realized that the logo reflects my theology of ministry. I designed this logo for the Hispanic Ministry in 2002 as part of an effort to draw attention to the unity of the church in its diversity. It was a concept I needed to express to the other leaders in my local church ministry. I wanted to express how I felt about the role of the Hispanic Ministry in relation to the other ministries. As I look at the logo today, I realize that it symbolizes the theology and spirituality of my ministry.

The core of my theology and spirituality of ministry is the Eucharist, and the shape of the logo reflects my devotion to the Body of Christ. I placed a golden circle around the drawing of the Eucharist to indicate that it has neither a beginning nor an end, in the same way that the Kingdom of God is timeless. Upon this drawing of the Holy Eucharist, I placed a cross that depicts people from different cultures. The people walk hand-in-hand in one faith towards Christ, who is the center. The Light of life of the Holy Spirit and Christ emanates from the center, shining on the earth, and the words in the light are "Unidos en la Fe" ("United in the Faith"). On the inner perimeter of the logo are the words "Ministerio Católico Hispano de las Parroquias de la Diócesis de Savannah" ("Hispanic Catholic Ministry of the Parishes of the Diocese of Savannah").

I believe that we Catholics, as a universal Church, must be inclusive and welcoming in the same way as Jesus. We should model our behavior after His actions. The purpose of my ministry is to unify cultures, build bridges, and see Christ in our brothers and sisters. I believe that the words expressed in Matthew 10:40 provide us with the formula to see the face of our Lord in each other: "He who receives you receives me, and he who receives me receives the one who sent me."

In my ministry, I, and anyone who ministers to the poor and marginalized, should avoid being judgmental by remembering the socio-economic and cultural-religious reality of the individuals, families and communities who need help. The focus of my ministry to all people, regardless of cultural background, is healing. When we minister to those people less fortunate than us, our actions communicate God's love.

Jesus' life, death and Resurrection give us the hope and the peace to endure our daily struggles. He was a migrant throughout his life, and His Holy Family provides immigrants today with a model to follow. I witness the strong impact that Jesus and His Family, especially the Virgin Mary, has on the immigrants whom I minister. They come alive in the

Church and are co-participants in the Kingdom of God, regardless of their background. I see the face of God in immigrants, whose respect for the Eucharist is so great, they feel unworthy of receiving it. In the absence of priests who speak Spanish, many Hispanic immigrants find it difficult to go to Confession.

The Catholic Church has been the center of life for all of us from Latin America. Many towns and cities developed around the presence of the Catholic Church, and a Christ-centered community is an important part of Latin American society. Towns and cities have a patron saint who serves as protection and an intermediary between the people and God. Hispanics are communal people, as evidenced by the number of single people who prefer to live together, sharing household responsibilities and partaking of the daily bread. Different families live together as well, and the parents and children share a bedroom. Community living is the *modus operandi* of the Hispanic immigrant in the United States today.

It is easy to understand the immigrant's need to feel welcome at the local parish. When immigrants do not find a Catholic Church, or one that is not welcoming, they becomes easy prey for the local non-Catholic church (Baptist, Episcopal, Lutheran or even the Jehovah Witness) that will try to satisfy the immigrant's spiritual needs to belong. This issue cannot be underestimated; if it is, the Catholic Church risks losing many Catholics to other faiths.

The theology of my ministry (action) is Christ-centered, and it moves me to build on the Body of Christ within the multi-cultural reality that exists in local diocesan churches. My ministry encompasses the entire Church, not just the Hispanic population. Collaboration is the key to success in ministry. The United States Conference of Catholic Bishops provides a guide for the development of "Lay Ecclesial Ministry" that is titled "Co-Workers in the Vineyard of the Lord." Within the context of this guide, I envision my ministry to the Hispanic Community and the Church as one that will bear the many fruits of unity in diversity. I thank God for the experiences that have brought me here.

My spiritual journey has taken me in so many directions, providing me with the opportunity to experience different cultures and learn new languages. Consequently, my spiritual ministry consists of a large tapestry of experiences from which my love of God flows.

As a pre-Vatican II child, I did not have a strong sense of God's presence in my life. My church's catechism program and my family's daily prayer of the Rosary enabled me to learn more about Christ and to develop a relationship with Him. Following Vatican II, I began to see and to experience God in the church and within my community. I feel blessed that Dominican priests and nuns served as my spiritual guides. Their influence was so profound that I considered becoming a priest. Once I met my wife Bessie, however, I realized that God had other plans for me—no way I could live without God's greatest gift to man.

I knew Christ was in me and felt touched by his divine presence early in my life. This knowledge was a spiritual awakening for me; it was the beginning of my spiritual journey. This journey took many turns, and I had a hard time listening to God for many years. I experienced many years of emptiness as I served in the military. In the beginning, there was not a Catholic at any of the places where I served. During my first tour in both Europe and the United States, it seemed that the Church I knew did not exist. When I was able to attend a church, I soon learned that it was Episcopal, Lutheran or Methodist. This time in my life was my first exposure to other denominations, and I became aware that there were no Catholics among the soldiers in the Anglo community.

Recently, I read again some of the letters I wrote to Bessie from Desert Shield/Desert Storm. Even though I felt the Lord speaking to me during this time, I did not listen to Him. Now, however, it is surprising to read and count the number of times I referred to God in the letters, as many as four or five references on a single page. The living God was with me all of the time, but I had not opened my ears, eyes and heart to Him. When I did open my heart to God, I began to serve Him in many ways, including as an Extraordinary Minister of Holy Communion and as the leader of a Communion Service. The Rosary quickly became my companion on many of the long trips I had to take.

After my military career, I continued to seek God in Spanish Mass again. I possessed a real thirst for His presence in my life. Since I did not feel comfortable yet worshipping in English, I used to drive more than sixty miles (round-trip) to South Carolina in order to be able to attend Mass in Spanish. My spirit ached for the Eucharist and the community life of the Catholic Church. I did not find a permanent parish until 2002; I still had to drive forty miles to attend Mass. It was about this same time that I heard God calling me and became aware of my spirituality. The language barrier faced by the English-speaking priest who celebrated the Mass in Spanish was one of the reasons that I feel God called me to serve Him. While the English-speaking priest did a beautiful job with the Spanish Mass, it was not the same experience as if a native-Spanish speaker had celebrated the Mass.

It took almost a year before I truly realized that God was calling me to ministry. The formation classes I took at the South Eastern Pastoral Institute in Miami helped me to understand what I was feeling. When the deacon who served the local parish asked me if I had planned to become a deacon, I realized at that moment my journey to serve God had begun. It was during this time that I understood that my calling to the diaconate would include my ministry as a bridge between the English-speaking and Spanish-speaking communities in Georgia.

I began to claim my God-given gifts during the diaconate formation program. The gift of languages I possessed was obvious, but the gift to be able to communicate with kindness was not. As the formation program progressed, I realized and accepted the others gifts I have, and I overcame the embarrassment of doing so. Since then, my ministry of selfless service to the community has been a source of blessings for Bessie and me.

Now, I have a new appreciation for the Paschal Mystery. I no longer fear applying what I have learned to my ministry. The Paschal Mystery has given me courage, and I use that courage to minister to people who feel overwhelmed by their circumstances. I remind them of our Lord's suffering. When people remember how much Jesus suffered, their problems, in most cases, do not seem as burdensome. Our problems, with the knowledge that God sent His only Son for our salvation, can seem less significant if we remember to turn to God for His mercy.

In working with people, I have become more patient and calm. I offer gentleness and a welcoming, positive attitude. My spirituality has developed through the years and is more in-tune now with the healing side of our ministry as servant leaders. Recently, I spoke to a community who did not enjoy a life-giving relationship with their priest. Upon reminding the members of the community to view their priest as the Good Sheppard, they gained a new appreciation for their spiritual leader and experienced peace.

I look at the whole process of my life until now and see that God had always been calling me to service. From the little kid with the guitar in the Christmas Choir to today, serving at Mass in church and the state prison, I understand that my call to service began long before I acknowledged it. In spite of my ignorance during the early years of my life, God did not abandon me.

My many experiences travelling the globe and living among people from different cultures groomed me to serve in the multi-cultural environment we live in today. I pray that I can help bridge communities into one seamless mystical body of Christ. My experiences in the social democratic country of West Germany, which consists of undocumented people from different nationalities, including Spaniards, Turks, Yugoslavians, Rumanians, and Arabs, prepared me to minister to people from a variety of cultures. In addition, the time I spent in the Middle East, where I experienced firsthand a theocracy and witnessed the devastation of war and desolation that an extremist state brings on its people. After these experiences, I visited Central America, where the poor and marginalized are mostly forgotten by the rest of society. Finally, I was born in the United States, and my time living in the United States enriches the many experiences I had abroad.

My spirituality enlightens my theology in prayer, in action and in words and policies. The action of my ministry meets with the prayerful, patient and my ever evolving spirituality. Action is the place where I apply my theology, and spirituality comes alive in the common realities throughout the Diocese of Savannah.

Since my brother deacons and I answered God's call, our lives have changed for the better. As we serve God's people and the Church, we join Him in his ongoing labor. I see the value of Ignatian spirituality, especially the presence of God in all things and the dynamic of outer→inner→outer, which I can apply to areas like immigration, poverty, domestic violence, victims of rape, alcoholism, substance abuse, and detainees in state prisons.

My ministry to people in South Georgia has provided me with a strong sense of Christ, who lives among us. I firmly believe that anyone who answers God's call to service will discover that the experiences of ministry are comparable to the Good News of biblical stories. It is exciting to be alive today in service to God.

I am grateful that my theology and spirituality of ministry continues to develop in the Diocese of Savannah. My ministry, especially my position as the Director of Hispanic Ministry for the Diocese of Savannah, is very much alive. When I began my job as the Director of Hispanic Ministry, there were only thirty-eight Spanish Masses in the Diocese. Now, there are forty-seven, and, soon, there will be one more. The first Spanish Mass I attended had twelve people. Today, this same Mass has four hundred worshipers; it is not uncommon for as many as six hundred people to attend this Spanish Mass.

May God bless and illuminate all who answer His call to serve Him and to love one another. Amen.

BIBLIOGRAPHY

O' Meara, Thomas F., O.P. *Theology of Ministry*. Mahwah, NJ: Paulist Press, 1999.

Deacon Bienvenido and Pam Perez
Our Lady Queen of Peace Catholic Church, Hunter Army Airfield

Bienvenido Perez, Jr.

MY THEOLOGY AND SPIRITUALITY of ministry are deeply rooted in my strong belief and conviction in God and our Lord Jesus Christ. God and his Son Jesus Christ are the source of my understanding of ministry. The scriptures describe in numerous events the main theological concept of ministry (love), and this concept is the essence of ministry and the basis of my understanding and practice of it. God made each of us in His image because of love, and love is the reason He sent his only Son to die on a cross for our redemption, for the forgiveness of our sins and our salvation. Scripture also tell us of the spirituality of ministry, which is completely based on the gift of the Holy Spirit. We are infused with the presence of our Lord Jesus Christ in our hearts and soul through the Holy Spirit, and we are given the opportunity through faith to share that spirituality with others as we minister to them. Now, I must admit that I have not always held a deep conviction and belief in God and his Son. I can call myself a cradle Catholic, but during several periods of my life's journey, I have not been a very good practicing Catholic. I have endured several life and faith altering events through the persistent love of God. Consequently, I have discovered anew my love and faith in God and his Son Jesus Christ. The first life-changing event for me was when my wife Pam and I began to attend Adoration regularly as a couple. This experience not only transformed our love for one another, but it also renewed my love for Christ and deepened my conviction to serve Him in any way that He desired. The second life-changing event was the development of my spiritual life based on "The Rule of Saint Benedict;" I am a Benedictine Oblate. Although I had lived most of my Christian life rooted in the principles of the Benedictine spirituality (Prayer-Work-Prayer), I had really never understood or knew that my spirituality centered upon St. Benedict. The third and last life-changing spiritual event for me on this faith journey occurred when I answered God's call to serve Him as a deacon. I must admit that I was somewhat reluctant, but what a blessing it has been for me.

Perhaps the most important theological concept I have learned about since I answered God's call to be a deacon is "Love." Love is the essence of God, and God is the essence of ministry, so love of God is and should always be the basis of the ministry of a deacon or anyone who serves God. In the Gospel of John, we find a beautiful and powerful passage that addresses the deepness of God's love for us, and it is also a verse quoted often by many Christians: "For God so loved the world that he gave his only Son, so that everyone who believes in him might not perish but might have eternal life" (John 3:16). For me, this passage exemplifies the essence of true love, and, when I reflect upon God's sacrifice, I cannot help but feel how much He loves me. This next passage brings to me the true manifestation of ministry and especially that of the deacon: "Put on then, as God's chosen ones, holy and beloved, heartfelt compassion, kindness, humility, gentleness, and patience, bearing with one another and forgiving one another, if one has a grievance against another; as the Lord has forgiven you, so must you also do. And over all these put on love, that is, the bond of perfection. And let the peace of Christ control your hearts, the peace into which you were also called in one body. And be thankful. Let the word of Christ dwell in you richly, as in all wisdom you teach and admonish one another, singing psalms, hymns, and spiritual songs with gratitude in your hearts to God. And whatever you do, in word or deed, do everything in the name of the Lord Jesus, giving thanks to God the father through him" (Col 3:12-17). I believe that these words embody the theological roots of ministry. They address many of the qualities that I believe make a good minister of Christ. First, it asks all of us who are believers to put on God's love, compassion, kindness, humility, gentleness, and patience, which we must feel before we can share that with others. It is unrealistic to share God's love with others if we ourselves do not feel it first. It is also unrealistic to share with someone our compassion, kindness, humility, gentleness, and patience if we do not recognize God as the source of those same feelings. The next two verses explain the real way in which we can share God's love with others: "bearing with one another and forgiving one another, if one has a grievance against another; as the Lord has forgiven you, so must you also do" (Col 3:13–14). Forgiveness is the calling card of any and every Christian. As Christ has forgiven us, so must we forgive others. I would also venture to say that forgiveness is not only a true testament of our love of God, but it is also one of the hardest things to do for any human being. To experience true love, one must experience true forgiveness. Christ so loved us that he was forgiving even until his last breath: "Then Jesus said, Father forgive them, they do not know what they do" (Luke 23:34). Jesus did not come into this world to remind us that we are all sinners; He entered this world to bring eternal forgiveness of our sins. Jesus suffered so that He could hold each one of us in loving arms and whisper, "Your sins are forgiven." In my ministry as a deacon, I pray that I will follow in Jesus' footsteps and be able to share Christ's forgiveness with other people.

The last few verses of the passage encourage us to let God's will rule our lives and to let our ministry flow from his love. This surrender is possibly the most difficult challenge that I have ever had to do. I am not sure that I have truly done so yet, but, as a result of the diaconal formation program, I am able to more clearly see God's will and have the strength and courage to follow it. The last verse of this passage is one of the most important for me, because it gives us a clear indication of how we must conduct our lives and, most importantly, live out our Christian lives: "and whatever you do, in word or in deed, do everything in the name of the Lord Jesus, giving thanks to God the Father through him" (Col 3:17). In other words, what we say and what we do should reflect what is in our hearts. If we look deep into our hearts, we will see God and His son Jesus Christ, the sources and summit of love. That is why I believe that Love is the most important theological factor when it comes to believing in and demonstrating this belief in God to others. God has shown nothing but love to the world, so if I am to call myself a believer of God, then I must also demonstrate that same love to other people. There is no mistaken love that emanates from a love of God, because its essence is compassion, kindness, gentleness, and patience.

I have experienced several life-changing, or life-giving, events in my life that have changed and shaped my spiritual life. The first of these events occurred when I became aware of Adoration. A dear friend, who is a devout Catholic, asked Pam and me to help him with a new project that he wanted to implement at our parish. As the President of the Parish Council, I invited my friend to speak to the Council about his idea, which was to establish Adoration at our church. The Council was very receptive and approved the expenditure so that a guest speaker could address the parishioners about Adoration. Again, my friend asked me to support him by attending the guest speaker's presentation on a Tuesday evening, and I agreed to support him. I want to stress and emphasize that, at this time, I was there only to support him in this endeavor, not to be a participant of Adoration. I was so busy at that time, I knew becoming involved with another endeavor would take time away from my many other commitments. I was there to show my support to him and because my lovely wife informed me that we would be there. I listened to the speaker talk about Adoration and what it entailed, and how we could set up a program to have twenty-four hour Adoration during the weekends. It was an interesting presentation, but to be honest, it did not move me enough to make a commitment. Besides, I felt like I did not need this spiritual "mumble-jumble stuff." But once again, I was outsmarted by my wife. By the end of the evening, and without my knowledge, Pam and I were signed up for an hour of Adoration the following Saturday. I could not believe it, and I was pretty upset about it because all I could think about was that I was not going to be able to sleep late on Saturday and that Adoration would interfere with my football-watching time. Pam prevailed, however, and we went to our (my) first Adoration. I can remember it like it was yesterday. I walked into this single-spaced room that had the Monstrance with the Body of Christ exposed, and I did not know what to do. It was a very awkward moment for me to say the least. I did not know if I should kneel first or sit. I was a very good actor and pretended that I knew what I was doing, but, in reality, I had no idea what I was supposed to do in that room. I sat there pretending to pray, but although I was saying the words, I was not really engaged in the prayer. On the other hand, my spiritually-mature wife seemed to be having a very meaningful conversation with God, and she seemed to be getting a lot out of that hour we were spending with God. When our hour was over, I was ready to bolt out of there never to return, but, once again, I was outsmarted by my wife, who had not only signed us up for the following Saturday, but all of the Saturdays on the sign-up sheet.

As I left the Chapel completely dejected and frustrated that I would have to return every Saturday, Pam asked me if we could go to breakfast and talk about our experience in Adoration. Well, I was not really interested in talking about my experience, but I was interested in breakfast. So, we went to a local breakfast restaurant, had a wonderful breakfast, and spent quality time together. Although I did not know it at that time, this event was the beginning of my spiritual development. It was the event that saved our marriage. Pam and I had struggled with our marriage for a few years, and nothing that we tried seemed to work in our favor. But, going to Adoration together and spending just one hour with our Lord, followed by a few precious moments together over breakfast, helped Pam and me to become closer to each other. I began to truly enjoy the one hour that I spent with the Lord in prayer with my wife next to me. It was during Adoration that I not only began to develop my spirituality, but I also began to develop my prayer life, too. I began to enjoy the one hour of quiet time with the Lord. In addition, I gained a new appreciation of praying the Divine Office.

Until this time, I had a spotty prayer life at best, but by spending this precious moment of silence with our Lord, for at least one hour a week, I began not only to pray more during that time, but also I began to pray more consistently throughout each day. Something was changing in me, and I did not know what it was at that time, but I can clearly see it now. The change occurred because I agreed to spend just one hour with our Lord in prayer. It was during this time of transformation in my life that I began to hear God's call to serve Him as a deacon. Ironically, I had been discerning my call without realizing that I was doing so. At first, I was reluctant to act upon God's call, because I did not see myself worthy of this task; I did not think I would be a good deacon, or so I had attempted to convince myself. With the help of my parish priest, Father Santry, I allowed God to convert me. One morning, I attended Adoration and had a conversation with God, in which I basically explained to Him that if He wanted me to be a deacon, that I would not resist this vocation anymore. I decided that if God wants me to be a deacon, then it would happen.

Fr. Santry and I began to meet more regularly after I had mentioned to him that I was thinking about becoming a deacon. He helped me tremendously to discern if the calling I felt was authentic or not. Once we discerned that God was indeed calling me to serve Him as a deacon, Fr. Santry began to help me with selecting a location where a program would be starting after my impending two-year assignment as a military helicopter pilot in Bolivia ended. To that end, Fr. Santry contacted Deacon George Foster, who is the Director of the Permanent Diaconate for the Diocese of Savannah. Now, it just so happened that after inquiring about formation programs in a number of other dioceses, we learned that a program would begin in the Diocese of Savannah at about the same time I would return from Bolivia. Perhaps it was Divine Providence, or, at the very least, interesting that Deacon Foster was a retired Army Officer who had a son who was also a helicopter pilot. To complicate matters, I did not have a return assignment to Savannah, so I was really pursuing something that was completely out of my control.

A year before I was scheduled to return to the United States, and at about the same time the application materials for the diaconate formation program were due, I spoke to my career manager about the possibility of finding an opening in Savannah. The immediate answer was a resounding, "No", but, upon further discussion and after checking other options, my career manager discovered that there was an opening in Savannah. Once again, was it a coincidence or the hand of God? At the same time that I was attempting to return to Savannah, I was also preparing my application to send to Deacon George Foster. It was a daunting task for a few reasons, the most challenging of which was that it was difficult for me to organize the materials I needed to submit while I was in Bolivia. In addition, I had never met Deacon Foster; all of our conversations took place by telephone. So, I was not even sure that my application would arrive before the selection of the candidates for the new class; another concern was that I was not sure if I had prepared the materials correctly. As it turned out, once I started the program, Georgia, who is Deacon Foster's wife, mentioned to me that I was the only candidate who had submitted all of the materials correctly the first time. The only reason I mention what Georgia told me is, once again, I cannot help but wonder if the application process for me was further affirmation from God of my calling.

My spiritual development and growth began when I agreed, albeit reluctantly, to spend an hour a week in solitude and prayer with our Lord. The time I spent in prayer, especially during Adoration, triggered the chain of events that have led me to where I am today in my faith journey. While my wife Pam was the reason I began to discover again my love for God, I deeply believe that God worked through her so that He could call me to serve Him. I obviously could not see what was happening at the time, but now I can, and I attribute this new perspective to the formation I received in the diaconate formation program.

When Dr. Pauline Viviano, who is a professor of theology at Loyola University of Chicago, asked my brother deacons and me during one of the classes in the formation program to define a "miracle," we were not able to do so. The most prevalent answer was, "a significant unexplained life event." Dr. Viviano asked us to re-think our understanding of what is a miracle, and she suggested that we consider as one possibility certain minor events that occur on a daily basis. Maybe we do not see them, because, after all, miracles are suppose to be large, life-changing events. While we look for the "big one," perhaps we miss the miracles of everyday life. I had never really thought of a miracle in that fashion, but it made me think of my own life, and whether I had missed miracles because I was looking and waiting for the big life-changing one. As it turned out, I can now recognize most, if not all, of the small miracles that have happened in my life, especially accompanying my wife, against my will, to my first Adoration. Without a doubt, Adoration, thanks to my wife, became the most significant life-changing miracle I had ever experienced. What is perhaps the most interesting aspect of this miracle, is that I have not returned to Adoration since. While I very much want to do so, none of the parishes where I have been a parishioner have had it.

I just noticed another small miracle as I was writing the previous two paragraphs: the many people who have affected my life and my faith journey. Their influence is a clear demonstration of God's Holy Spirit at work in my life. He has brought different people (spirits) into my life at different times in order to guide me to where I am today. I can state with all of the confidence in the world that I am sure that He will continue to place certain individuals in my life who will guide me in this faith journey until I am reunited with Him in Heaven.

The next life changing event, or dare I say life-giving event, was the development of my prayer life, which is due to my attending Adoration. Now, I think that I can consider this part of my ministry one of the most significant ones, because it has led me to a more complete understanding of my relationship with God. Prayer has helped me to persevere: "Persevere in prayer, being watchful in it with thanksgiving" (Col 4:3). Prayer, and more importantly being able to communicate with God through prayer, has allowed me to endure even in the most of difficult of times. I needed to learn how to pray, much in the same way that the disciples asked Jesus to teach them to pray: "Lord, teach us to pray just as John taught his disciples" (Luke 11:1).

When I began to attend Adoration, I was very nervous and apprehensive because I was not sure how I should be praying. Fortunately, however, I had begun to pray the Liturgy of the Hours (or so I thought) years before my encounter with God during Adoration. In addition, I was also very familiar with the Rosary as a member of the Knights of Columbus. Consequently, I began to pray the Rosary and the Liturgy of the Hours each time I went to adoration, and soon I found myself truly enjoying the time I was spending with God in prayer. I also started to learn more about praying the Liturgy of the Hours, and I discovered the Benedictine tradition.

In another moment from God, or small miracle, I met Fr. Lee, a Benedictine priest who was a Reserve call-up who worked at Hunter Army Airfield. He introduced me to the Benedictine monks of the local Benedictine high school, and I began to develop a good friendship with him and many of the Benedictine monks. I also had the opportunity to forge a great friendship with the Prior, Fr. Jude Brady, who also became my spiritual director, and without him I might not have continued the diaconal formation program. With the help of these monks and many more, I began to explore the Benedictine Spirituality and realized that I truly enjoyed that type of spirituality. Furthermore, I felt very comfortable with the Morning and Evening prayers. A year later, Pam and I became Benedictine Oblates. Because of this chance encounter (coincidence or the hand of God?), I was able to discern my calling to the diaconate and discovered a deeper spiritual journey never before experienced. I begin every day with Morning Prayers, and just the other morning came across the following intercessory prayers that reflect beautifully the spirituality of ministry:

Our Savior has made us a nation of priests to offer acceptable sacrifice to the Father. Let us call upon him in gratitude:

> Preserve us in your ministry Lord.
>
> Christ, eternal priest, you conferred the holy priesthood on your people, grant that we may offer spiritual sacrifices acceptable to the Father.
>
> In your goodness, pour out on us the fruits of your Spirit, patience, kindness, and gentleness.
>
> May we love you and posses you, for you are love, and may every action of our lives praise you.
>
> May we seek those things which are beneficial to our brothers, without counting the cost to help them on the way to salvation.

During my ministry as a hospital chaplain, I prayed these prayers often before the start of each day. Praying the Liturgy of the Hours, Morning and Evening Prayers has opened a door into the heart of God through which I had never walked before. I have developed a sense of the Holy Spirit and see God's movements in me and in others in a way that I had never witnessed before.

One of my most memorable experiences from the diaconal formation program was how the Holy Spirit affected my brother deacons during the five years we prepared for ordination. I am so blessed to have had the opportunity to meet and become friends with such beautiful human beings. Each and every one of them has brought something special to the formation experience, and I have learned, and continue do so, much from them. A truly blessed event that occurred during the years of the formation program was my participation in a retreat that one of the other candidates, at the time, organized in Savannah. If he had invited me to participate before I entered the formation program, I probably would have declined. I immediately said, "Yes," though. While I had never served Christ in this way before, I felt His strength and possessed the confidence that I would be able to create a presentation for the college students who attended the retreat. On the day of the retreat, I had the opportunity to meet twenty young people who had decided to spend a weekend with each other and with Christ. It was a great experience for me! It was wonderful to see young people choose to spend their weekend with Christ. I was worried that I would not deliver an effective presentation or even connect with these young people, but I was completely wrong. As a matter of fact, they made the experience easy and enjoyable because they made me feel welcomed. The students' enthusiasm, commitment, and passion taught me a lot about Christ and His love for each one of us. The weekend I spent with the students was proof that Christ's message is very much alive in the minds and hearts of the next generation. The students I met that unforgettable weekend know Jesus and live His message of love everyday of their lives.

It has been a true blessing to be able to learn so much from each and every one of my brother deacons. My brother deacons possess a myriad of talents and gifts, and they utilize them in numerous ways to spread the Good News. When I answered God's call, I did not foresee the positive impact my vocation would have upon my family. My wife Pam completed her four-year degree in Religious Studies from St. Leo University, and, currently, she is the Catholic Coordinator at the post chapel at Hunter Army Airfield. My daughter Angie is a religious education teacher, alter server, and she is also very involved with our youth group. Not only have I experienced the movements of the Holy Spirit in my life, but my family has as well.

In conclusion, the core of my ministry is "Love." The development of my prayer life continues to have a profound impact upon my growth as a Christian. As a result of prayer, I am a much more spiritual person who is now capable of discerning the movement of the Holy Spirit, not only in my life, but also in the life of other people. I would like to conclude by sharing this prayer, which I pray daily, that I found on the Internet several years ago:

A DEACON'S PRAYER

O Jesus, Eternal Priest, you have called me to be a deacon to your people. Give me the ability to serve them so that they will be aware of your glory. Let me see the good in your people and inspire me to recognize and use the talents you have given them. Help me to be prayerful without being sanctimonious. Release me from every desire to be all-important and teach me the glorious lesson that occasionally I may be mistaken. I ask for a growing humility that I might more fully understand what you want me to do. Protect my family and let me not be neglectful of their need and protect me, O Lord, from myself. Amen.

BIBLIOGRAPHY

The Catholic Study Bible. Eds. Donald Senior and John J. Collins. New York: Oxford University Press (U.S.A.), 1990.

Deacon James and Arlene Roberge
St. Patrick Catholic Church, Kathleen

James Roberge

WITHOUT A DOUBT, I embarked on one of the most rewarding endeavors of my life when I answered God's call to serve Him as a deacon. God has a dream for me. Can I accept it? Spirituality is discovering/discerning the dream and living it to the MAX in a Ministering Church, "living the God Life." Fr. Thomas O'Meara's book *Theology of Ministry* had a profound impact upon me, and, for this reason, I organize my essay around several passages upon which I expound my feelings and thoughts.

"Ministry is an action" (153):

I used to see ministry as something that we did to help others in the church or in need. There was more than a hint of personal satisfaction from doing what I did; it was quite the ego boost, for example, to sing in church and to hear people tell me how good I was. Then, thank goodness, I had a Pauline experience. I discovered during attendance at cantor school that I had changed and that I was, from that moment of enlightenment, being called to serve God as a minister. One who was called by the Spirit of God to serve using the talents he gave me.

"Ministry is not a badge, not an office, not a cliché but a spectrum of various concrete and helpful services to grace" (147):

Ministry is not a job. It is not a paycheck. As a matter of fact, I have served as director of music and liturgy at my parish since 2001 in an unpaid capacity. It was my choice. I have been reimbursed from my effort not in monetary terms, but, rather, in the grace of God and a closer relationship with Him. It is service to others guided by the spirit.

"Ministry is not a hobby for everyone but a permanent decision to be both servant and sacrament" (257):

Ministry is what God calls us to in Isaiah 6:8, "Here I am" or Psalm 40, "Here am I." It is recognition of the call of God to serve him. In addition, it is recognition of the old answer in the Baltimore Catechism: to know, love, and serve God in this life and in the next. I can only do that when I am open to the will of God and when I follow the guidance of the spirit.

Many people were surprised by my Myers-Briggs results of the Introverted Thinking with Sensing (ISTP) analysis, even my wife Arlene. I was not. I am frightened by new situations surrounded by strangers. I am able to "fake it till I make it" through my acting ability. In more comfortable situations and situations, where I am expected to be loud and in charge, I can rise to the occasion. Yet, sometimes, I fall back in exhaustion.

Do I see my development directed by the Holy Spirit? Very much so. There have been so many trying times in my life, yet when I look back and reflect on them, I see divine intervention in every fork in the road. The following quotation from Fr. Michael Cooper, who was one of the professors during the formation program, serves as a constant reminder that God is with me: "Out of death and dying in everyday life, God opens up new life, new hope, new possibilities in amazing and unexpected ways." God has led me to where I am today; I have walked, sometimes run and sometimes dragged my feet. I know that because of the free will God has given me, however, it has been my choice. I look for new life, new hope and new possibilities in death and dying. I ask others to look for them as well and to share them.

Do I see the Christ in myself that others seem to see in me? I pray in song. I use many songs like "The Summons," "Open My Eyes," and the St. Louis Jesuits' "Take Lord Receive", their musical "Suscipe,"[1] to reflect on my relationship with God and with others. In Cursillo, we hear of a statue of Jesus that was recovered in a church destroyed by a bomb in Germany in which the hands are missing, but, in their place is a sign: "He has no hands but yours." I also hear echoed in John Kennedy's inauguration speech, "God's work must truly be our own." At times, I do see the Christ in me, and I thank God for the recognition of it. I do not do so in a boastful way, but as an appreciation of the spirit of God within me.

After I did the Strengths, Weaknesses, Opportunities and Threats Analysis, my strengths, as determined by me and other people, were that I am a good husband and father, and a good provider. My sense of humor helps me overcome rough spots and keeps me sharp as I make sure I am an active listener. In addition, I am a very good liturgist and church musician. I am really energized by liturgical planning and being able to stay in the moment as the planning come to fruition. I have a charism for being able to see the final results of things I am planning, and I am able to know what works and what might not work. I have very good situational awareness and am able to make adjustments to ensure that things work out as they should. While I do appreciate the residual joy out of a job well done, I do not do it for my own edification or to receive praise. I serve God in my ministry as a deacon because He called me, and I answered, "Yes."

"Ministry comes from the Spirit of God and from the individual's personality" (199):

Since I answered God's call, my life has undergone many changes, some of them have been to who I am, while other changes are reflected in what I do.

---

1. *Suscipe* is the Latin word for *receive*, and it is the title of St. Ignatius Loyola's well known prayer

For example, I taught an RCIA class a short while ago. My wife Arlene had a look of unbelief, but she also realized the changes I am experiencing. In a way, it was her personal realization of my changes that she could share with me. I began to read the Scripture readings for the upcoming Sunday during the week and to ponder how they affect me. What could I share with the people who worship with me? Then, I compare and contrast my interpretation with that of the homilist. How did I do? Am I getting it? I read and hear the word of God differently now, and I have a new sense of responsibility with each reading. I know that people will be looking to me to "break open" the Word. I know and believe that God is present in the homily and that He will be present with me when I preach.

Do not get me wrong. I am scared, because I do not want to disappoint. Fortunately, I have been blessed over the years with many wonderful role models of faith to guide me on this part of my journey. Arlene and I did not meet a deacon until 2000, but we had the pleasure of becoming friends with three deacon couples (the deacon and his wife) at this time. Each one of the couples has been a mentor and guide to Arlene and me in our journey. They have given us strength when we have needed encouragement, and they have served as role models and examples of how to live a life of grace and faith.

The word of God also strengthens me. The following examples provide guidance for me in my future ministerial life:

> Deacons must be dignified, not deceitful, not addicted to drink, not greedy for sordid gain, holding fast to the mystery of the faith with a clear conscience. Moreover, they should be tested first; then, if there is nothing against them, let them serve as deacons. Deacons may be married only once and must manage their children and their households well. Thus those who serve well as deacons gain good standing and much confidence in their faith in Christ Jesus (1 Tim 3:8–10, 12–13).

> Let your love for one another be intense, because love covers a multitude of sins. Be hospitable to one another without complaining. As each one has received a gift, use it to serve one another as good steward of God's varied grace. Whoever preaches, let it be with the strength that God supplies, so that in all thing God may be glorified through Jesus Christ (1 Pet 4:8–11a).

> Contribute to the needs of the holy one, exercise hospitality. Bless those who persecute, bless and do not cure them [. . .] Rejoice

> with those who rejoice, weep with those who weep. Have the same regard for one another; do not be haughty but associate with the lowly (Rom 12:13-21).

I also find the readings in the Liturgy of the Hours very appropriate for ministry. On the day our class was installed as lectors, the reading for Saturday morning was from 2 Peter 1:10-11:

> Brothers, be all the more eager to make your call and election firm, for, in doing so, you will never stumble. For, in this way, entry into the eternal kingdom of our Lord and savior Jesus Christ will be richly provided for you.

I was privileged to be the leader of prayer that morning. The words jumped out on this reading, as each of my brother deacons (candidates at the time) realized we were making a commitment. St. Peter was asking us to make this commitment. The reading reinforced for all of us that the word of God is truly a now event. It speaks to us now and in everyday life, because it is the divine word of God.

"THE PAST NEVER FULLY DISAPPEARS; OLD FORMS ARE NOT FULLY REPLACED; THE NEW MUST BE BOTH INCARNATIONAL AND TRADITIONAL" (138):

As ministers and people who answer the call of God, it is important to be ever mindful of the past when we serve God and His people. Just as important, however, is to remain open to the movements of the Holy Spirit so that we can recognize in what direction God is guiding us. Recently, for example, my parish began praying the *Pater Noster* during Mass. While we are not planning to offer the Tridentine Mass, we, nevertheless, want to be sure that we relearn and, in a sense, reclaim, a part of our Catholic heritage.

There have been times in my life when I seemed to have hit a pinnacle of success in ministry, especially in liturgy. Even then, however, I know that I can be more effective. I know that mistakes happen, because, after all, we are human, but if our heart and focus are with God, whether we feel that we are effective or not will not matter, as the effort will be a worthwhile one.

According to O'Meara, ministry is (1) doing something; (2) for the advent and presence of the kingdom of God; (3) in public; (4) on behalf of a Christian community; (5) as a gift received in faith, baptism, and ordination; and (6) as an activity with its own limits and identity existing within a diversity of ministerial actions" (141). Ministry also is, in my opinion, an endeavor to which we are all called to take part in the best we can. In Cursillo, one of the open talks is on the laity, and this talk seeks to communicate the important concept that anyone who professes to be Catholic *is* the Church. They have a role to play, and perhaps their role is more important, due to the large numbers, than the role of the clergy. There is a plurality of ministries, a diversity, which deepens our connection to one another as we enjoy the benefit of all beings belonging to the one body, one spirit in Christ. In this diversity we see relationships between the ministries in power, humility, and holiness (O'Meara 168).

Most ministries in the Church are public, but how they are recognized or classified can be stretched a bit. My former parish in Maine held an appreciation dinner each year for the people who served as ministers, defined as anyone who contributed his or her time and talents to the church. The pastor sought to recognize the people who volunteered in one capacity or another on a regular basis. He did not consider making a cake for a bake sale a ministry. How does one define ministry? According to O'Meara, ministry is not inclusive of every activity for a very good reason: "When everything is ministry, ministry fades away" (190). I believe there is a definite difference between doing something where the principal motivation is earning a salary and an action performed selflessly and in the name of God.

Whether a person realizes it or not, God calls everyone to service: "Everyone has a vocation! [. . .] Every Christian has a vocation to ministry, to serving the kingdom of God [. . .] There are ministerial vocations other than those to religious life and priesthood" (O'Meara 210).

Personally, I see it as my *Suscipe*. I agree wholeheartedly with O'Meara's assertion that God calls everyone to serve Him.

O'Meara emphasizes the communal aspect of ordination: "*Ordination is a sacramental liturgy performed by a Christian community and its leaders during which a baptized, charismatically called, and professionally prepared Christian is commissioned into a public ministry within and on behalf of the local church*" (218; italics by O'Meara). In ordination, a person receives a specific grace from the Spirit through the witness and affirmation of the assembly. The members of the assembly are the witnesses in the same way that people witness a wedding ceremony between a man and a woman. Unlike other ministerial duties, ordination is permanent. Ordination is a public declaration of a ministry that is a life-long commitment to serve God and His people at all times.

"CLEAR MINISTERIAL IDENTITY BRINGS [...] DISTINCTION AND DEMAND FOR COMPETENCE" (180):

I have developed, in large part due to O'Meara, a new appreciation for the importance of ministerial education. Ministers should receive proper training so that they can perform their respective ministries to the best of their ability and in a way that reflects God's love and grace. I am an advocate of more commissioning/presentation of the ministers in the parish so that the entire assembly can pray for the people who answer God's call.

"'MINISTRY' IS NEVER A 'JOB.' ALL THOSE SERVING THE PRESENCE OF THE SPIRIT ARE BOUND BY A HIGHER CALLING, A SPIRITUAL LIFE" (196):

Since I entered the diaconal formation program, I have reflected often on spirituality, including St. Ignatius of Loyola's *Spiritual Exercises* and several other spiritualities about which I have learned. O'Meara notes the connection between ministry and spirituality: "Spirituality for ministry is a bridge between the baptized and their services" (225). There is no gift or ministry without love, and ministry that is not performed with love is not ministry. O'Meara also mentions the vital role of love in spirituality: "Motivated by love and enabled by grace, the ministry serves others" (229).

"MINISTRIES ARE INEVITABLY THE RESULT OF GRACE ACTIVE IN PEOPLE AND IN THEIR INDIVIDUAL STRUGGLE TO BE MINISTER IS THEIR SPIRITUALITY" (231):

Recently, I taught an RCIA class on the Holy Spirit. I was able to use O'Meara's book to reaffirm the importance of the Holy Spirit in each of our lives, especially in the call of ministry that comes to us from the Spirit of God. My spirituality is grounded in the Cursillo movement. I see in it a balance of piety; study and action that emphasizes silent time with God and the importance of public ministry. The Cursillo movement calls us to be accountable for and to each other in our small sharing groups. We begin each gathering with a prayer to the Holy Spirit, and, then, we talk about the moment we felt closest to Christ during the past week. In this way, we embrace Ignatian Spirituality, according to which God is with us, and around us, in all that we do, and the Gospel is a now event. In

Ignatian Spirituality, we also witness "the context of ministry is contemporary life" (260).

The liturgy is such a powerful spiritual part of my life as well, because it is a time during which we all share the Paschal Mystery. The communal nature of the Mass is all-inclusive, as the worshipers include the people in attendance, Catholics around the world, and especially the people in Heaven.

Music is very important to me. I obtain great peace in singing and playing in praise of God, especially during the liturgy. There was a time when I utilized my musical gifts for self-aggrandizement. Today, however, I understand that my gifts are meant to serve God and His people during the Mass or wherever I may sing or play an instrument. I find great solace in religious music, most especially in Catholic music. Whether I listen to Gregorian chant or contemporary songs with reflection on Scripture, religious music brings me the peace that I know only God can provide.

According to O'Meara, some of the problems that the Church faces today are due to ministries that lack spirituality. In ministries that are performance based, like music, for example, the theatrical nature replaces the intended purpose of sharing one's gifts to glorify God. I try to make each rehearsal more than music practice. We always start with prayer, and the other musicians and cantors and I read the next Sunday's readings between the songs we rehearse. If time allows, we also discuss questions pertaining to the readings. I find that this focus upon Scripture reminds us that we are not just at Mass to perform, but, rather, we provide support to the gathered assembly and are active participants in the liturgy. The Mass is for the ministers, too.

Another way in which my parish attempts to focus upon spirituality in ministry is by encouraging everyone, but especially ministerial leaders, to attend Cursillo. As of last year, everyone who was in a position of responsibility was a Cursillista. This participation in Cursillo makes for a more spiritual community.

I need structure in my spiritual life, and I found it in the Liturgy of the Hours. I make a sincere effort to pray at least one of the Offices each day. In addition, I try to reflect upon the readings of the day and to attend daily Mass.

Since the moment I returned from cantor school to this day, I have never felt that what I do in service to God and His people is about me. I have surrendered myself to God, and He has revealed to me the glory of my sacrifice, which I express in my own *Suscipe*:

> Take Lord, receive all of me. I was given all from you.
> My thoughts, my talents, my material goods are all from you.
> Lord, I surrender to your will. You Win.
> I neither request nor desire nothing of this world.
> Only let me serve You.
>
> Your love and your Grace are all I need.

Every time I let go and give myself up to God, I am rewarded. The more I give, the more I receive. I conclude my essay with one of my favorite Bible verses: "This is what Yahweh asks of you: only this, to act justly, to love tenderly and to walk humbly with your God" (Mic 6:8). I hope I am able to do what God asks of me.

BIBLIOGRAPHY

O' Meara, Thomas F., O.P. *Theology of Ministry*. Mahwah, NJ: Paulist Press, 1999.

Deacon Joseph and Mary Soparas
St. Teresa of Avila Catholic Church, Grovetown

Joseph S. Soparas

As I write down my thoughts about the journey I have been on since I answered God's call, I find that I am just as enthusiastic and excited about it as when it first began. I have watched my fellow diaconate brothers grow in their relationship with The Blessed Trinity and the Church. I have also seen the positive effects this journey has had on our home life and my wife's approach to her own spirituality.

As a result of the academic component of the formation program, we are better versed in the theology and praxis of our Church than when we started. To my way of thinking, we are better prepared to venture out as deacons and to fulfill our mission involving ministry of the Liturgy, the Word and Charity. We have more confidence in our ability to explain and teach our faith. What follows is a brief overview of the courses that constituted the academic component of the diaconal formation program.

This journey began with our Aspirancy Year, a spiritual retreat meant to bring us closer to God and to set the tone for the next few years of study. Our text was *Moment by Moment, A Retreat in Everyday Life*, which consisted of selected Spiritual Exercises of St. Ignatius of Loyola designed to help us allow the Holy Spirit to bring our hearts and minds into an environment that would closely follow Jesus in faith, love and spiritual freedom. With guidance from the Holy Spirit and an understanding and patient teacher, spiritual director and friend, this purpose was accomplished. We began finding God in all things. The work was about to begin. Going back to school after thirty years, however, and in a different type of subject, was a bit daunting.

CyberCulture: New Challenges for Pastoral Ministry introduced us to many ways to utilize the world of the Internet for ministry and evangelization. We learned different ways to use the Internet in our ministry, to enhance our presentations and to make our time more efficient. I experienced this efficiency when I was the Chairman for our Capital Campaign at Saint Teresa of Avila Catholic Church. I had to communicate, sometimes daily, with committee members, the Pastor, Church office and the fund raising company. I was able to compose one message and reach many at all hours of the day and night. Questions, proofing, and decisions that needed answering the same day were sent early, and a resolution was reached the same day, instead of days or a week. We could not have accomplished so much in such a short period of time without the Internet. We often talked in class about the advancement of technology in spreading the Gospel and making it available to a larger audience. I saw evidence of this potential in our Diocese a couple of years ago when Bishop Boland organized a Catholic celebration for Pentecost at the fairgrounds in Perry, Georgia. The auditorium held 3,000 Catholics from all over the Diocese. Mass was held in the auditorium and very large monitors hung from the ceiling so all could see the Mass and other speakers on the main stage.

History of Christianity provided us with the necessary information to better understand how the Church began, the historical course it traversed, the Church's successes and failures, and understanding of the Reformation and Christianity's emergence into the twenty-first century.

The Old Testament and New Testament courses consisted of a thorough analysis of major themes and events, as well as a comprehensive presentation of the background material one needs to appreciate truly the genius of the Bible.

Christian Ethics took us on a journey to find the deepest part of conscious to explore natural law and the character of the person. We studied cultivated virtues and attitudes in relation to the morally-good life a person leads. The question asked at the beginning of the course, "What sort of person should I become because I believe in Christ?" was explored in depth.

World Religions began with the philosophy of each religion we studied, which included the Native American Indian's Sacred Pipe of Black Elk to Gandhi to Sufism and the meditative techniques of each religion. Another aspect of the class explored enculturation, the process by which the Church can use and assimilate the culture of the people into the Gospel Message.

Theological Foundations explored the pre- and post-Vatican II theology found in Catholic thinking, and the controversies they stirred in the Church. We learned how the Holy Spirit continues to work among us to keep Christ's word alive and up-to-date in today's world.

In *Worship, Liturgy and the Sacraments*, we explored the history of the Sacraments, their theology, how Vatican II affected the Sacraments and the Church, and how symbols, rituals and narratives are involved with formation of character, knowledge and imagination in the human being. Deacon George Foster, the Director of the Permanent Diaconate for the Diocese of Savannah, also provided valuable practical advice related to administering the Sacraments.

We began by reading *Ministry Burnout*, by John A. Sanford, in the last course of the program, *Theology and Spirituality of Ministry*. This text explores nine pitfalls facing ministers that can lead to psychological and physical problems for the minister (5–15). I have witnessed ministerial burnout in priests and the lay ministers in our parish. Some of the lay ministers succumbed quickly to the rigors of parish politics and their ministerial roles. For others, it took a couple of years.

Another text, *Theology of Ministry*, by Thomas F. O'Meara, O.P., begins by taking a historical look at Church ministry and how it has evolved from the early days of Christianity to the ministerial role of postVatican II. He takes us back to the beginnings of Christianity and notes how early Christian communities had to pull together to survive physically and spiritually. The Apostles, Saint Paul, disciples of Jesus and the deacons helped to shape and guide these early communities. Charisms of the individual members were brought together to create a community strong in faith. There was no hierarchy of ministers.

Times change, and as the culture of the world and the environment proved more favorable for Christianity, the theology of ministry changed as well. I believe that the Holy Spirit had been at work directing the Church and its leaders since the Spirit descended upon the Apostles at Pentecost, but the culture of the times and Man's free will created a Church ministry that was hierarchical, courtier and in some cases corrupt. The gap between the Church hierarchy and the laity was widening. To offset this side of the equation, there is the development of the monastics and mendicants, ministers the people could turn to for guidance and who kept the Church alive during these troubling times.

As time moves on, the theology of the Church really stays the same for centuries. The hierarchy of the Church moves away from auspices of the kings and emperors, but the separation of the clergy and laity remains; consequently, faith formation for the laity is not a pressing ecclesial issue. Pneumatic correction (the movement of the Holy Spirit), though, is still at work and influences a pope who was to be only an interim figure head to invite a few of his colleagues over to the Vatican for a meeting that would last a few years. The ideas and theology of people like Yves Conger and Karl Rahner were now embraced. The Holy Spirit had succeeded through the efforts of Pope John XXIII, his successor Pope Paul VI and Vatican II in opening the Church to a new era of cooperation between the ordained ministers and the laity. The long suppressed priestly ministry of the laity, given at Baptism, was now embraced. There was a revitalization of the whole Church from the Vatican down to the smallest Catholic parish. Events of Vatican II probably had their effects on other religions, even if it was only to announce to the world that the Catholic Church was alive and well and taking its role in the world community seriously.

The shift from the priest and religious-centered parish to a more diverse ministerial model is fueled by a shift in biblical, historical and theological perspectives. Through Baptism, we share in Jesus' role as priest. We are a Spirit-driven and grace filled Church, and the charisms given to us by God and manifested through the guidance of the Holy Spirit are meant to help all promote the Kingdom of God. As Jesus told us, we should love God with our whole being and our neighbor as ourselves. The Kingdom is love of God and each other, and the Beatitudes are an essential component of this ambience of peace and joy. If only we could live like that, but, unfortunately, too often, free will leads us astray.

O'Meara points out the six characteristics of ministry, "(1) doing something; (2) for the advent and presence of the kingdom of God; (3) in public; (4) on the behalf of the Christian community; (5) as a gift received in faith baptism, and ordination; and (6) as an activity with its own limits and identity existing within the diversity of ministerial actions" (141). It has taken some time for the spirit of the Vatican II documents, especially their resounding support of active lay ministries, to become normative at the parish level. The ministry of the Church, through the efforts of the Holy Spirit, Vatican II and the bishops has changed. Pre-Vatican II, a priest was the spiritual, financial and physical head of the parish. Sisters and Brothers were involved with teaching, nursing, or social action in the community, and the laity was a passive participant in church life. Vatican II changed this parish model to one where the priest is at the center of the concentric circles (O'Meara 157) of ministry. Today, the laity is active in many different ministries of the parish, including youth and adult education, faith-sharing Scripture groups, Rite of Christian Initiation of Adults, and Catholics returning home. Lay ministries are very much alive in my parish, where the parishioners truly embody, and in a variety of ways (Parish Council, social outreach, evangelization, parish finances, etc.), O'Meara's characteristics of ministry.

The post-Vatican II generation seems to be experiencing a theological and spiritual rebirth, much in the way that early Christians underwent a transformation after the Resurrection. Jesus, through the Holy Spirit, helped the early Christians manifest in their lives the grace and love of God and neighbor needed to survive. Today we have the Scriptures, the Holy Spirit and a new understanding of the dignity of Baptism. In addition, we have the tools not only to survive, but to grow and move onward with the Kingdom of God.

I believe my spirituality and decision to answer God's call emanated from the influence of the Holy Spirit and the charisms I received from

God. Baptism allowed the Holy Spirit to give me the graces that would help me later in life. Until I began the diaconate formation program, I never really had discerned how I reached this point in my life. Over the last few years, however, when I look back, I can see a time when I had a choice between a religious life and raising a family. God gave me the opportunity to choose, and I chose a family. God has been good to me and my family, and He used my decision to serve Him as a husband and a father as a training ground for the future, namely my ministry as a deacon. By choosing this path and staying close to God, I have found success in my family life, professional career, Church life and the Knights of Columbus. With the success, however, I also experienced tragedy and failures. I am not perfect, and the road I walked was not always the straight and narrow. In spite of my personal weaknesses as a human being, my unwavering love and faith in God enabled me to remain close to God and the Church. God accompanied me on my journey and nourished me spiritually by exposing me to many different people and scenarios that have taught me to be responsible and caring. My wife has been a God-send and a true partner. I love her dearly. My children and grandchildren have always held a special place in my heart. People are important and make a difference in our lives, and all of the success in the world does not mean a thing if the people you meet in life only associate negative experiences and feelings with you. The success is a result of helping people on their journeys and bringing Christ to them. Even though I answered my call to be a husband and a father, God still called me to serve Him. The road that I followed to this point has not been an easy one, but the experiences have taught me a lot.

A recent article in our Augusta, GA. newspaper stated that many people are choosing not to attend church. This statement arose from a poll conducted by a marketing research organization, Barna Group, and the three main reasons for not attending or joining a church were: (1) the hypocritical behavior of church members; (2) the perception that the church's beliefs or expectations are too strict or intolerant; and (3) the sense that church and church membership are irrelevant in maintaining a relationship with God. The poll stated that these findings reflected the sentiment of twenty-five per cent of the Catholics interviewed. Parishioners' lack of involvement in church life is one of the problems facing the Church today. How are we to keep the church community intact in today's climate? How can we reach the youth whom families and the parish have trained spiritually over the years to remain active in the Church after they are grown and leave home? It is important, in my opinion, to involve people from an early age in church life through programs geared to fostering church life as a lifestyle. Young Life, a Protestant-based youth movement, has been successful with the youth for many years. It takes committed parents and ministers to remain engaged in the religious growth of young people as they grow older. It is not enough to provide the youth with entertainment and sports activities. While these worthwhile activities feed the mind and body, engaging spiritual programs must be developed to feed their souls.

Anyone who answers God's call to service must not lose sight of the valuable influence of the Trinity in their lives, especially when they encounter challenges of a divisive nature. Laity and clergy alike are called upon to serve God and His people in a manner that always emphasizes the healing purpose of ministry. We must remember that our service to God is inextricably linked, therefore, to the feelings, perceptions, and personalities of the people to whom we minister.

BIBLIOGRAPHY

McKevie C. Samantha. "A Day of Rest." *Augusta Chronicle (Religion)* November 24, 2007.

O' Meara, Thomas F., O.P. *Theology of Ministry*. Mahwah, NJ: Paulist Press, 1999.

Pistone, John. "Spirituality of the Deacon Couple." *Deacon Digest* (January–February 2007).

Sanford, John A. *Ministry Burnout*. Louisville, KY: Westminster John Knox Press, 1982.

Deacon Albert and Debbie Sullivan
St. Mary on the Hill Catholic Church, Augusta

Albert Sullivan

As I write this essay, I cannot detach who I am from what I feel, especially as I write about my views on spirituality and the changes I have experienced since I answered God's call to serve Him as a deacon. I am forty-eight years old, and my wife's name is Debbie. We have two wonderful children, Jared and Erin. My married/family life is a gift. In my wildest imagination, I cannot imagine a more fulfilling and life-giving marriage and family life. Debbie and I have been married for nearly thirty years, and God's grace has been a true blessing to both of us. I am the third of five children, and both my mother and siblings live in the same city as I. My father passed away a few years ago.

The idealistic family life of Ozzie and Harriet was not what I experienced growing up. My father was a recovered alcoholic who struggled mightily with his disease, and my mother always provided a stable home environment. While I always had been impressed with the way that my mother maintained family unity and harmony, it was not until I had my own family that I realized the incredible blessing that she was to my family. My mother was the rudder to a very unsteady boat that the "SS Sullivan" was in those days. Much of who I am today is due in very large part to her influence.

It took me a while to give my father a break, but now I understand that he did the best he could. Looking back upon the more difficult years, it seems that we both matured at the same time. Before he died, our time together was very peaceful, and I am grateful for these moments with him. My life prepared me for who I am today as servant of God and His people. I guess the Lord does work in mysterious ways.

I met Debbie in college, and we married after we had dated for four years. Debbie's faith, and that of her family as well, was and still is very strong, and it did not take long for me to know that I wanted to share in their joy. Their lives were God-centered, and they lived their faith. I wanted to experience the blessed life they lived, so I converted to Catholicism in 1983.

Religion, at least not in the formal sense, did not play a significant role in my family's home while I was growing up. My earliest memories are of AA meetings, twelve-step programs, and one-day-at-a-time mantras. Our prayer was the Serenity Prayer. To this day, my mother still reads from the Alcoholics Anonymous' Big Book and practices the twelve steps.

As I recall the first meeting of the diaconate formation program, I remember thinking that the beginning of my diaconate journey was also the continuation of a journey that I had been on for many years. I am not sure when this journey began for me. Certainly, I have a recollection of when I first heard about the permanent diaconate and of realizing that an indescribable desire seemed to be leading me toward something that was bigger than me. I spent the Aspirancy Year of the formation program looking backwards, trying to reconstruct the steps that inspired me to answer God's call, and looking forward, attempting to foresee the steps, and possible missteps, which awaited me.

I have no doubt that God placed me in Debbie's life, and I also believe that, through Debbie, God guided me to the Church. Debbie never expected me to attend Mass with her or tried to convince me to do something I did not want to do. All I had to do was be a witness to the joy and fulfillment with which Debbie lived her life to know what my life lacked.

I stayed very busy during the first years following my entrance into the Church. In addition to the birth of our children and the awesome responsibility I felt of being a good Christian role model, I sang in the choir, taught religious education, served as an Extraordinary Minister of Holy Communion, and was a member of several parish committees. As the children grew and attended the parish school, our lives seemed to revolve effortlessly around the Church and our faith. I finally had achieved the Ozzie and Harriet lifestyle. I found myself participating less in parish life due to the increasing demands placed upon Debbie and me as Jared and Erin grew older. It was also during this time that Debbie began to work at the parish school that our children attended, and, later, she served our church as parish secretary. Debbie's position at the church gave me the opportunity to get to know the priests, brothers and nuns of the parish. As I watched these men and women over the years, I began to find myself drawn to them and to the selfless way in which they seemed to lead their lives. In addition, I had the opportunity to see them without their collars and habits, and I realized that they were human beings like me who had answered God's call to serve Him and His people. I attribute this attraction that I felt to the priests, brothers, and nuns to the great respect I had for them, but I also believe God was speaking to me about my vocation.

The devotion to my spiritual life for a long time centered upon my gratitude for the wonderful family life God had given to me. Today, I realize that God does not require payback for what He provides us with on a daily basis, because He loves each one of us unconditionally and only asks that we love Him in return. When I think about the unconditional love I feel for my wife and my children, I understand how God loves me, too.

When I first learned about the permanent diaconate program, I felt attracted to it. My life seemed too busy, however, to pursue it. During this time, I found myself incredibly passionate about becoming a deacon when I witnessed deacons assisting at Mass, but I also would lose that enthusiasm once the new week began. Eventually, however, I experienced waning enthusiasm less and less and began to think more and more about the possibility of serving God as a deacon. As I think back on it now, I see that God was very much working in my life. When Deacon George Foster, the Director of the Permanent Diaconate for the Diocese of Savannah, who also served at my church, told me that a new formation program was about to begin, he said without hesitation that he thought I would make a good deacon. What had been an idea in my head was now becoming a real possibility. When I began to take inventory of the situation, including the number of sins I had committed, the pros and cons of the program, and whether I was worthy to serve God as a deacon, I decided that the diaconate was not my vocation. God thought differently, though. During a farewell reception for our parish priest, Deacon George handed me an application to the formation program. After all of the tug of war I had gone through, it came down to God, through George, calling me to follow Him so that He would make me a fisher of men.

Even as I began the formation program, I was not completely comfortable with the chances of my completing it. Perhaps the constant questioning and discernment were positive reactions to the tremendous commitment I would make if ordained. On the good days, I rode the crest of that wave, feeling at peace with my decision to go forward; on bad days, however, the feelings of inadequacy simply exhausted me.

I have always been a "big picture" sort of person, and that approach has served me well in my professional and personal life. I know it takes both vision and attention to detail to achieve a successful balance. I have always surrounded myself with people who provide that balance to my broad-stroke approach to life. The benefit of looking ahead is that you give yourself the time to anticipate, plan and implement. The cut to that double edged sword, however, is you are continually planning your next move, taking only a moment to savior the now. My initial approach to the diaconate journey, quite understandably, given my big picture inclinations, was to approach this process incrementally: year one, year two, etc. What I found, however, was that I was running out of toes to stump. God does not work on my timetable, but I knew that He was always present, providing me with direction and guidance. It seemed that I was doing all of the heavy lifting, but I supposed that was how it should be.

The bond that I developed with my deacon brothers and their wives (deacon couples) before ordination provided me with much strength and comfort. I have always considered myself something of a lone wolf. I grew up in a large family that, for the most part, did not allow many people to be a part of our inner circle. While I certainly developed friendships as a child, as a teenager, and as an adult, I did not have many friends, and they, for the most part, did not become a part of my personal space. I understand that the dynamics of a large family are such that family members can fulfill the need for friends, but I also feel, perhaps cynically, that we utilized the large family dynamic as a defense mechanism. In spite of any seemingly difficult challenges I faced growing up in my family, I can say with assurance that today I am a very happy person who is outgoing. I suppose, growing up in a large family, I did not feel the need for companionship outside of my parents and siblings.

A minister, I believe, should be a person whose life models the Two Great Commandments. I truly do love God with all of my heart, with all of my soul, and with all of my mind. I find it a challenge, however, to always love my neighbor as I love myself. While I have no ill will for others, I simply have never been a person who invested himself so much in other people to the point that I could say that I loved them. The young, the old, and the disadvantaged, however, are three groups of people for whom I have much affection. God challenges me to extend myself as I serve Him, and I am grateful that He recognizes that I am capable of much more love.

While I had never been a person to speak openly about myself, and especially not my religious beliefs, the community dynamic of the diaconate formation program proved to be the setting I needed to feel more comfortable. As a minister now, I am much more at ease talking about my relationship with God. I appreciate hearing about the spiritual journey of other people, and I realize that my journey is capable of providing comfort and strength as well.

As I look back on the five years that Debbie and I spent with the other deacon couples during the formation program, I wonder why I felt so comfortable around the men and women with whom we shared our journey. After all, we were a large group of people of different ages, backgrounds, and cultures. The unifying thread was our love of God. Each of us knew that a deeper relationship with God would translate into something greater than we imagined. In addition, I appreciated the honesty and openness with which the deacon couples shared their life stories. The courage with which some shared the tragic aspects of their lives impressed me greatly. As I reflect on what I heard and saw from the deacon couples, I realize that ministry, especially mine as a deacon, is all about sharing openly different experiences, both good and bad, with other people. We must give of ourselves in order to help other people discover themselves and appreciate how special they are in God's eyes.

Deacon George and Georgia Foster
St. Michael's Post Parish, Ft. Gordon

George Foster

Epilogue

One's spiritual and academic life's journey never ends this side of glory. I make this statement in a very positive sense as I have been privileged, as was my wife Georgia, in witnessing the growth of nineteen men whose spiritual and academic journey you have read. These men and their spouses have come from different backgrounds in terms of culture, ethnicity, education and professions. The acceptance and support of each other was instant. Each knew why he was called, and each reached to embrace and encourage one another, knowing that their journey would not just be an individual one, but a collective one.

As I read each article in this reflective book, my own belief in each man was a testimonial of the calling of the Holy Spirit to the diaconate. I was privileged to be able to talk to each privately as they shared their own thoughts, anxieties, and uncertainties, which were emotions and feelings that are most natural, with me. I was able to recall with them in community my own journey and my own emotions leading to ordination and my ministry.

During their formation I stressed to each that the diaconate ministry is one of "getting your hands dirty," to work with the outcast, the homeless, the drug addict, the prisoners, the dying, the lonely, the alcoholic, the sexually abused, the abused housewife, and the forgotten. For this is ministry in the raw. And the model deacon of the above was our Lord Jesus, who embraced all unconditionally with love and forgiveness.

In reading each paper from these men, I believe they have shaken loose of the "old man" and taken on the "new man" with a deep spirituality, but also with a realistic look at the Church in the secular world of today. They can engage today's society in accepting people where they are in their own journey in life and also share with each a deeper love of themselves, the love of the wonderful gift of life, and make the journey with them. Not being judgmental, but also at the same time, sharing God's love for each unconditionally.

This book has been a desire of one man, Deacon Michael McGrath, who wanted each of his deacon brothers to share their journey as how each has grown as a man, as a deacon, as a husband, as a father, and as a friend. I know that those who read this book will be gifted by the prayerful words these nineteen deacons share with each reader. I pray that the wish of Deacon McGrath will be fulfilled and that we all will be a better person because of it.

The journey continues with each day as we discover who we are, the full meaning of the beautiful gift of life, the many gifts we have received, and the knowledge that fullness of life is in loving, sharing, crying, and laughing with others, knowing that when this earthly journey ends, the other side of glory awaits us in the fullness of God.

www.ingramcontent.com/pod-product-compliance
Lightning Source LLC
Chambersburg PA
CBHW051930160426
43198CB00012B/2095